D0717923

U-BOATS
AT WAR
Landings on Hostile Shores

U-BOATS AT WAR

AT WAR
Landings on Hostile Shores

Jak P. Mallmann Showell

Ian Allan
PUBLISHING

First published 2000

ISBN 0 7110 2721 8

All rights reserved. No part of this book may be reproduced or transmitted in any form or by any means, electronic or mechanical, including photocopying, recording or by any information storage and retrieval system, without permission from the Publisher in writing.

© Jak P. Mallmann Showell 2000

The right of Jak P. Mallmann Showell to be identified as author of this work has been asserted by him in accordance with the Copyright, Designs and Patents Act 1988.

Published by Ian Allan Publishing

an imprint of Ian Allan Publishing Ltd,
Terminal House, Shepperton, Surrey TW17 8AS.

Printed by Ian Allan Printing Ltd,
Riverdene Business Park, Hersham, Surrey KT12 4RG.

Code: 0011/B

Photographic Acknowledgements

The photographs in this book come from the U-Boot-Archiv, including the Walter Schöppe collection, from the author's collection and from people listed at the end of the Introduction.

The maps come from IMSI's Master Clips Collection, 1895 Francisco Blvd East, San Rafael, CA 94901-5506, USA

Above: At low tide, a number of U-boat wrecks can be seen in the estuaries of southern England. These do not date from World War 2 but were lost shortly after World War 1 when they broke their tow while on the way to breaker yards. Two such boats are visible from a public footpath along the banks of the Medway near Kingsnorth Power Station. They are lying about 400 metres north of a long, derelict oil jetty and about one kilometre from the shore. The jetty can be made out in the right of this photograph and the U-boats appear as a dark blob to the right of the ship in the far distance. From this vantage point, they can be seen quite plainly with binoculars. Walking out to them would be suicidal because the entire area consists of a fine silty mud, too soft to take a person's weight.

Half title: The bows of a Type VIIC at sea.

Title: U302, a Type VIIC with early conning tower design speeding through Norwegian waters for the benefit of a film camera.

Front cover: Type VIIC boats with earlier type of conning tower design. Otto Giese.

Back cover, top: A Type VIIC on sea trials with box-like rainhoods over the hatches still in place.

Back cover, centre left: Men lying exhausted on the characteristic wide deck of a Type IX.

Back cover, centre right: U178 under Korvkpt Wilhelm Dommes, a very long range boat of Type IXD2.

Back cover, bottom: Type VIIC boats with later type of conning tower design. U-Boat-Archiv, Cuxhaven, Germany

Contents

Three men of *U379* pictured in 1942.

Introduction:
U-boat Landings on Hostile Shores

Spy mania, lying dormant in Britain since 1918, was quickly rekindled by the eruption of World War 2. Eccentrics who did not fit into the standard pattern of life were confronted by officials to have their privacy scrutinised; nuns with unusual habits and large Boy Scouts with the wrong woggles were arrested; foreigners were interned and public information and private communications were censored more tightly than ever before. The frenzied grip of desperation also gave rise to a long chain of reports about U-boats landing on isolated parts of the British coast. Many of these stories were probably invented to boost sales of local newspapers or to help whip up a fighting spirit in those who were still reticent about following their government into another programme of officially sanctioned mass murder.

The strange point about these accounts is that first-hand eye witnesses disappeared exceedingly quickly and anyone searching for information was left with hearsay. This was easy to find because there were loads of people who had neighbours with friends, whose cousins had met chaps in pubs, who had overheard their boss at work say that the stories were true. What is more, some reports were even supported by such indisputable evidence as pictures of wrecked houses with captions saying that they had been demolished by gunfire from submerged U-boats.

Eye witnesses would want us to believe that intrepid U-boat men photographed insignificantly small English bridges a couple of kilometres inland, that they visited British pubs for recreation, that they brought secret agents ashore, kidnapped members of the Home Guard, and also carried out a vast number of other daring feats. After the war, this hysterical fascination for Winston Churchill's most feared weapon was further fuelled by retired officials who invigorated their autobiographies by publishing the wildest of questionable information. According to such books, it would appear that the dreaded U-boats participated in some even more extraordinary escapades than the earlier hearsay wanted us to believe. Stories of landings on British, American and other soil were surpassed by U-boats which had carried gold, art treasures, high ranking Nazi officials and troupes of naked dancing girls.

There are stories of U-boats having landed in Sussex, Dorset, Devon, North and South Wales, several places in Scotland, Blythe, Whitby, Norfolk, the Thames Estuary, Dymchurch, Dungeness and no doubt many more, but in all cases it has been impossible to trace the U-boats responsible. Those landings

Above: The problems with clandestine landings on the English south coast were immense, despite the coast lacking the obviously dangerous rocky features of the west. Much of the shoreline is guarded by natural vertical walls, such as the White Cliffs of Dover, and many of the flatter areas are exceedingly muddy or overlooked by a large number of houses. This shows a rebuilt German patrol boat which went down near Richborough Power Station, between Ramsgate and Sandwich, long after the war. Despite efforts to raise it, the mud held it firmly in its grip, keeping the boat there to rot away.

The east and south coasts of England are still littered with a large number of derelict observation posts, such as this one near Folkestone. During the war they made it difficult to approach the shores without being seen.

which have been recorded with dates took place at times when there were no U-boats anywhere near the landing sites, which would suggest that agents had been ferried over the Channel by fishing boat or yacht. This was not terribly difficult because weather frequently provided ideal cover for such brief clandestine crossings. What is more, a German secret service yacht remained undetected at sea until 1944.

After the war, while this fantasy of frequent U-boat landings was establishing itself in the minds of the masses, stories of secret submarine bases also started germinating in a variety of publications. Some of this intrigue has been used for firing enthusiasm into tourists at mundane seaside resorts where U-boat anecdotes added glamour to muddy beaches and worn-out amusement arcades. The thought of German agents being landed from decrepit fishing boats just could not match the attractive fascination offered by a supposedly secret U-boat. The concept of a secret refuelling base on Fuerteventura where Martin Bormann was supposed to have lived presented an even greater attraction and is still helping to fill tour operators' coaches.

Many of these stories are 'supported' by confidential documents so secret that they cannot be released to the general public and only a few fortunate authors have had the advantage of glimpsing an accidental sight of them. One of these classified sources, a list of clandestine U-boat bases, is worthy of further consideration. Yes, such a book did exist. The whole concept sprang to life during World War 1 when the light cruiser *Dresden* escaped superior British forces after the Battle of the Falkland Islands by seeking refuge in the myriad channels around Tierra del Fuego. Many of the inlets there had not been charted and local sympathisers, with knowledge of those waters, made it possible for the ship to evade the Royal Navy until the lack of fuel and provisions brought an end to an epic voyage.

By the beginning of World War 2, the German navy had made a determined effort to be ready to help commanders who might find themselves in similar situations, where they needed shelter in out-of-the-way locations, bearing in mind that there were still a good number of uncharted islands in those days. This took the form of a valuable, secret and most comprehensive book, with the title of *U-Plätze* or 'U-Places', an expression which could very easily be corrupted to 'U-Bases' and from there to 'U-boat Bases'. However, the 'U' has no connection with U-boats. It stood for *Unterkunft* meaning refuge or accommodation.

Mentioned in the list were desolate locations like Trinidade, about 1500km east of Rio de Janeiro, where an inland lagoon is supposed to be connected to the sea by a natural underground tunnel. After the war, when some of this information leaked out, the place became an ideal candidate

Above: An old lookout tower on top of the canal cutting near Dymchurch in Kent, which has now been demolished, with the Redoubt in the background. The Redoubt has the distinction of having been constantly occupied since it was built during the middle of the 19th century and is still used by the army to this day. Two secret agents, Charles van der Kieboom and Sjoerd Pons, landed close to this tower during the night of 3/4 September 1940, but they were brought over by fishing boat, rather than a U-boat. They were discovered and arrested by soldiers shortly after landing. Most of the better local historians have reported this sequence of events correctly, but there are a good number of false accounts stating that the landing took place from a submarine.

Above: During the war, there was already a sea wall protecting the low-lying marsh around Dymchurch, but it was nowhere near as high as it is today and much of the Romney Marsh shores looked more like this. Of course, there would not have been many fishing boats during the war. Some of the round Martello Towers were used during the war as observation posts. Indeed, the first V1 flying bomb was reported from one near Dymchurch which has now been demolished.

Above: The Dymchurch Redoubt near West Hythe, where the two agents landed in 1940.

Inset: One of the Martello Towers built during the Napoleonic era to defend the English coast. There were a good number of them, some used as observation posts, when German agents landed in World War 2.

for making into a clandestine U-boat base. However, the German book was so secret that no one read the passage saying that the tunnel was inaccessible even to small boats because of rocks blocking both ends.

During those immediate postwar years it was virtually impossible to separate fact from fiction because the Allies had confiscated German war records and classified them as secret. Information which was allowed to filter out was strictly controlled and obviously showed the Allies in the most favourable light. The later release of documents did not alleviate the problems with clandestine U-boat missions because many of the events had not been recorded in log books. Instead, information was passed orally to the high command when the boat returned to port. And since many boats on such missions failed to return, but are known to have made landings before being destroyed, there are indeed quite large blanks in the histories.

In addition to an acute absence of information, research for this book has turned up a rather strange abnormality concerning a few of the boats which were lost. It should have been possible to reconstruct some details of their last operations from logs of the U-boat Command, but in at least two cases the records for the period in question have been tampered with by removing the vital pages. This naturally leaves the suspicion that something significant may have occurred. It would seem somewhat pointless for the U-boat Command to record details and then crudely eradicate the evidence by tearing out the appropriate pages. So could this have been done after the war by the people who captured the documents?

These problems with the records have underlined the great danger that any further accounts given here will only add more fantasy to the already high pile of dubious documents. This is

Above: Although the Dymchurch Redoubt looks idyllic, the water along this shore still hides a forest of obstacles which are visible only at low tide. During the war, the defences would have been more extensive and laced with mines and barbed wire.

all the more real because there appears to be quite a substantial army of individuals who enjoy misleading others by fabricating documents and coming up with the weirdest of stories with the hope of selling them to the gullible — and there has been a rapid increase in the volume of this sort of deceptive information since the advent of the Internet.

Among the most blatant forgeries was a postcard and several personal documents supposedly written by the author's father shortly after he had allegedly landed secretly in the United States. A photocopy, accompanying the invitation to purchase the material, contained sufficient mistakes to indicate the passages had probably been put together by an American rather than a German and the forgery could be exposed. However, even experts have been misled by good quality counterfeits.

In view of this abundance of false information, I have avoided newspapers, magazines and sources with high prices. Much of this book is based on log books and first-hand accounts from the International Submarine Archive (U-Boot-Archiv) in Cuxhaven and I am most grateful to Horst Bredow, its founder and director, for guiding me through his comprehensive collection.

I should also like to thank Graham Bloxall, John Gallehawk, Gudmundur Helgason, Philip Kelly, Bill Love, Michael Lyons, Carole Patton, Elizabeth Walker and Franz Selinger for supplying information.

Above: Two other agents, brought over from Boulogne by the same fishing boat which carried Kieboom and Pons, landed near this spot on Dungeness. The houses in the distance were built after the war and both José Waldberg and Carl Meier landed unobserved in splendid isolation.

Above: They hid their luggage and radio in the remains of an old wrecked fishing boat, not very far away from where this one was stranded after the war.

Above: From Dungeness the two agents made their way inland along this road. It was single track during the war. The two gravel pits beyond the bushes in the distance were excavated later as well.

Above: One of the agents made his way to Lydd, where he was arrested trying to buy something to drink, and the other one was picked up shortly afterwards near Boulderwall Farm, which can be seen on the left in this photograph. Today this is part of the RSPB nature reserve. During the war, the whole of Romney Marsh as well as the other coastal regions were restricted areas and people living or visiting there required special passes. This, together with the isolation of the small marsh communities, made it easy to spot 'foreigners' in places such as Lydd, where everybody knew virtually everybody else.

Chapter 1
Irish Fiascos

Prewar efforts to establish clandestine links between the German secret services and the IRA (Irish Republican Army) fizzled out partly as a result of Hitler's assurance that there would be no armed conflict with Britain until the late 1940s at the earliest. However, the IRA's resumption of bombings on the British mainland, just a few months before the outbreak of the war, prompted German Military Intelligence (Abwehr) to consider re-establishing contact with sympathetic elements in Ireland. This became an even more attractive proposition once the war started because it was thought that the IRA might be willing to help disrupt the British armaments programme. Unfortunately, the vital link with the decision makers in the IRA had not been set up and in September 1939 the Abwehr asked the Naval High Command whether submarines could be used to land their agents to organise such a liaison.

KptzS (Kapitän-zur-See) and Kommodore Karl Dönitz, who by September had been promoted from glorified flotilla commander or Flag Officer for U-boats to Commander-in-Chief for U-boats, did not like the proposition. His uncommitted but agreeable fobbing off did not work and just a few days later powerful forces in the High Command were back, asking for the Abwehr's plans to be given highest priority. At this stage several people started working on different parts of the same plot without knowing of each other's existence and therefore produced a rather vague and disjointed set of plans, which resulted in the most chaotic operational consequences later on.

The U-boat Command's Operations Department produced a set of blank orders because it was not yet known which boat would carry out the mission. The main instructions were:

1. Two agents are to be landed in Ireland, somewhere near a railway line with connections to Dublin.
2. The choice of the exact location is left to the U-boat commander.
3. This mission must not be discussed by anybody anywhere. The crew may not even talk about it while on board the boat. Anyone breaking this order will face a death sentence.
4. The agents are to be landed in a rubber dinghy of the type used by the Luftwaffe and this must be destroyed immediately after use.

Someone in the Operations Department must have known that this last instruction was going to be a major problem and added that the submarine's wooden dinghy could be used if conditions proved too difficult for an inflatable. The reason for the afterthought was that inflatables tend to float on top of the water, rather than in it, and therefore are more susceptible to winds. Sometimes it is virtually impossible to move them in any direction other than the one in which the wind is blowing. As a measure of consolation the U-boat Command emphasised that it did not matter if the dinghy was lost in the process.

The commencement of the first operation coincided with the rather singular opportunity of *U37* leaving for the North Atlantic. *U37* was one of the early long-distance boats, which had been in position off northwest Spain at the beginning of the war and was then hurriedly brought home to be made ready for a possible wolf pack attack. Her commander,

Heinrich Schuch, was replaced by Werner Hartmann, who had been a flotilla commander for the past year. The idea was that he should act as an on-the-spot tactical commander to lead the first wolf pack offensive, but the U-boat Arm did not succeed in getting sufficient boats into the Atlantic and this role fell flat. However, as a large submarine *U37* was suited for carrying passengers and the new commander was experienced in making out-of-the-ordinary decisions.

It was a bitterly cold January day in 1940 when the agent, Ernst Weber-Drohl, turned up in Wilhelmshaven disguised as a war correspondent and carrying a couple of large suitcases. Approaching the age of 60, he was already looking forward to peaceful retirement, rather than an audacious escapade into the wilds of Ireland, and he did not appear too enthusiastic about the prospects. It could well have been that he also brought his own personal problems along. His radio operator certainly failed to get on with him and had dropped out two days earlier, saying he could not cope with this acidulous character. The Abwehr did not have a great choice in agents. Although many spoke English, there were hardly any who could do it with a convincing Irish accent. Consequently the absent radio operator was not replaced and Weber-Drohl was trusted to accomplish the mission on his own. He knew the country quite well and was acquainted with local customs because he had toured there a few years earlier, visiting country fairs with his own strongman act.

Nobody blinked when he came on board. There were a few curses about his heavy cases, which had to be turned on end and then only just squeezed through the hatches, but there was nothing to make the passenger stand out in a crowd. War correspondents had already become a fact of life and the young crewmen in the boat guessed that anyone more agile would be used for more demanding jobs than taking pictures inside a submarine.

Venturing out from Wilhelmshaven on 28 January 1940, *U37* battled through a dense field of thick ice floes in the Jade Estuary. It was a period of intense cold, when even the salty coastal waters had frozen into a white rocky desert. Several boats had already failed to cross this barrier and had to return to have new propellers fitted. This time everything went well, but it was not until *U37* was rocking on the high waves of the ice-free Atlantic that Hartmann told his men about their guest's real identity. At the same time everybody was ordered to sign a piece of paper informing them about the special secrecy and making it plain that anyone found talking about the venture, whether outside or inside the boat, would face a death sentence. This was not only new to the men, but also somewhat unusual. However, none of them had been to war for long and the threat was washed down just like every other bitter pill.

Weber-Drohl experienced quite an ordeal within the confines of the stinking submarine. His mission had not been given priority and therefore Hartmann first took the opportunity of attacking and sinking two small freighters. The 1,365grt (gross registered tonnage) *Hop*, bound from Bergen to Middlesbrough, was almost too small for a torpedo, but uncooperative waves, combined with possible retribution from the air due to the proximity of the Scottish mainland, made

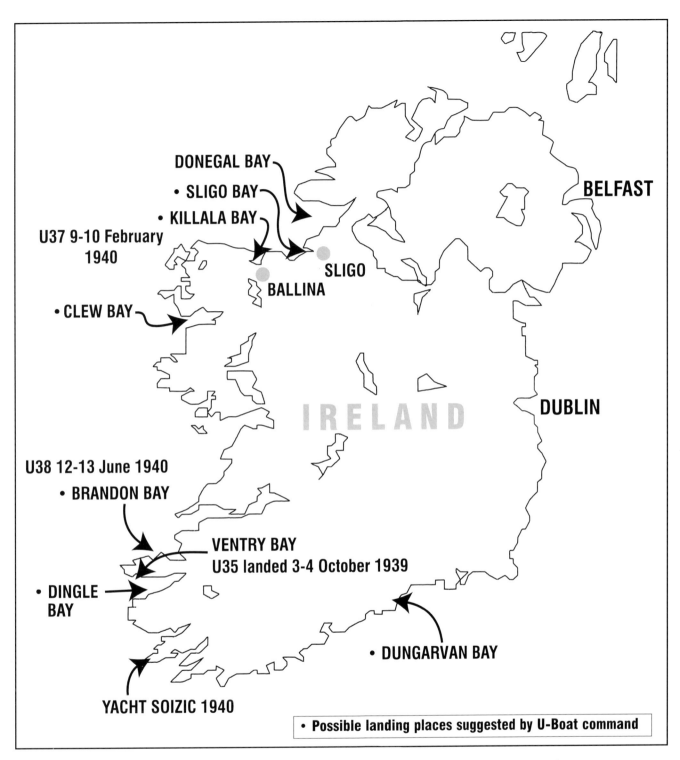

DONEGAL BAY

• SLIGO BAY

• KILLALA BAY

U37 9-10 February 1940

BELFAST

SLIGO

BALLINA

• CLEW BAY

IRELAND

DUBLIN

U38 12-13 June 1940

• BRANDON BAY

VENTRY BAY
U35 landed 3-4 October 1939

• DINGLE BAY

• DUNGARVAN BAY

YACHT SOIZIC 1940

• Possible landing places suggested by U-Boat command

him shy away from engaging with the deck gun. The second ship (the 4,330grt *Leo Dawson*) was attacked during the evening of the same day, 4 February 1940, just a few miles east of Sumburgh Head on the Shetlands. From there Hartmann swept through the main shipping lanes of the North-West Approaches before making for the Irish coast.

Once within sight of land, Hartmann and his men first took bearings on a number of easily identified landmarks to confirm their exact position. This had hardly been accomplished when a steamer, far out in Donegal Bay, forced the boat below the waves. The intrusion did not matter a great deal because the coming of daylight would have made it impossible to have remained on the surface. A steady southeasterly of force 3–4 was thought to have been to the U-boat's advantage because it was blowing from the land and therefore unlikely to create too much turmoil on the beaches. Unfortunately, no one on board seemed to have been acquainted with the Atlantic swell washing along the west Irish coast and Hartmann found that even the sheltered side of Sligo Bay was sporting an incredible surf, far too rough for an inflatable or a dinghy.

A scrutiny of the situation through the periscope made Hartmann decide that it would be better to creep further west, with the hope of finding a more suitable location in Killala Bay. This was not the first time that this area was used for clandestine landings. Almost 150 years earlier the French General Humbert had landed there with about 1,000 troops to help in an Irish rebellion. It was dark by the time U37 reached Killala Bay, but at least there were fewer rocks and the warm waters of the Gulf Stream prevented any traces of the ice which had hampered progress in the German Bight. According to the chart, Weber-Drohl was even going to land on a comfortably firm sandy beach.

So far everything had gone off with military precision, but now Hartmann's decision to go ahead with the landing sparked off an unrehearsed pantomime. It quickly became apparent that the small rubber inflatable from the Luftwaffe was designed to carry one, perhaps two, half dead airmen who had baled out without a great deal of kit. It obviously was not big enough for a well-built secret agent with suitcases. When the submarine slowly submerged, allowing the dinghy to float off on the waves, it was plain that the heavily laden rubber air bag was not going to go anywhere very far, other than perhaps turn over and spill its contents.

Had he been watching the sequence in a cinema, Hartmann would have laughed out loud, but now all eyes were turned on him to take the next positive step. The U-boat Command had already suggested the alternative and the wooden dinghy was brought up from its storage box under the deck planking. The idea of doing all this so close to the Irish coast did not appeal, even if the country was neutral, without any navy to worry about. Lookouts constantly scrutinised their surroundings. The second launch had hardly got under way when the U-boatmen realised that Atlas, the ex-strongman, had not been taught how to handle small boats. The manner in which he waved the oars about made the seamen think that he was more likely to head for America than the nearby beach.

Jumping to the rescue, the third watch officer, Leutnant-zur-See (LtzS) Hans-Günter Kuhlmann, took pity on the floundering agent. His request for permission to leave the boat was first taken as a joke and Hartmann hardly reacted, making only a few positive grunts. For reasons the crew had not yet been told about, he watched apprehensively as the cockle-shell craft disappeared into the blackness. A few specks of light in the far distance suggested the land was indeed inhabited, although the remoteness of the beach was further emphasised by the dampness of the cold breeze. Hartmann did not like it. Time dragged by and the silence was almost more frightening than the deafening blast from a depth charge attack. It seemed to be an eternity before Kuhlmann returned with an empty boat. Cold and wet, but with a broad grin indicating that everything had gone well, he was eagerly helped back onto the deck. His first voyage in a U-boat had given him a unique opportunity to make his mark, something he could never have done had he remained as torpedo officer aboard the heavy cruiser Blücher. His impressive display of seamanship instantly promoted him from the green new boy to a highly respected leader. Sadly, this colourful character was killed in action a few years later as commander of U166.

Dripping in front of Hartmann, he described how he grounded the boat, jumped into the waves, carried the luggage out of reach of the water and then even gave the little fat man a piggyback. So far Hartmann had kept quiet, but now was a good time to tell Kuhlmann that the U-boat Command had given the strictest of orders that none of the crew was to leave the boat. Dönitz did not want to risk losing his men in harebrained operations and specially emphasised that the agents were not to be helped ashore. Hartmann was highly relieved to have his third watch officer back and pleased that Weber-Drohl arrived without hardly having got wet. However, none of them knew that the suitcase containing the all-important radio was not designed to be transported in small dinghies. It could not cope with even a slight infusion of seawater and the radio had now ceased working.

Weber-Drohl reached his contact from the IRA, who had earlier visited Hamburg, and he even survived at large for three months, though it was hard for a foreigner to stay undetected in the tight-knit Irish communities. Consequently, in April 1940, he was arrested and interned, but all that still lay far in the future when the men of U37 made for the vastness of the Atlantic to broadcast the code words signifying success in their part of the mission.

The second attempt to land agents in Ireland had nothing to do with espionage nor links with the IRA. Instead it fell to the Abwehr to establish a weather station in the Republic. This was important because many of the prewar sources providing raw meteorological data had shut down or, if they continued broadcasting, it was in code, and it was difficult to forecast weather in Europe without their input. In view of this the Abwehr trained meteorologists and then dispatched two of them to Wilhelmshaven.

Kptlt (Kapitänleutnant) Heinrich Liebe knew they were coming. He already had a similar set of instructions to those handed earlier to Werner Hartmann. His U38 was an identical type to U37, having been designed during the mid-1930s for long-distance voyages. However, leaving Wilhelmshaven in early June 1940 made this a considerably more pleasant undertaking. Unfortunately, Liebe did not record any details of this mission in his log. There is only one reference on 12 June 1940, saying simply 'Special Mission'. From that one can conclude that he succeeded in landing both agents. Very little else of note happened during the previous days, the boat had not been involved in combat and the only entries concerned the weather which had varied around the moderate mark.

This time U38 carried two agents. One of them, Willy Preetz, had married an Irish girl long before the war and acquired an Irish passport in the name of Paddy Mitchell. This was not too difficult because even long after the war it was still perfectly legal for anyone to call themselves by any name and that name could be used on official documents in preference to the original words from the birth certificate. So, although very little is known about Willy Preetz, the change in names could well have come about for social reasons rather than clandestine intent.

The other agent, Walter Simon, was a considerably more problematic character inasmuch that he had served the Abwehr before and had even been arrested in Britain and deported. This did not affect his status in Ireland, but did mean that he was probably known to the authorities there. The Irish government was keen on keeping up good relations with London, to prevent giving any excuse for the country to be occupied by British forces. So it is likely that there was reasonable liaison in the field of criminal investigation. Although the almost 60-year-old Simon had been given a new identity as an Australian, this did not prevent his early arrest. In fact, it could well have been that the authorities knew about his arrival because he was picked up exceedingly quickly.

His colleague, Willy Preetz alias Paddy Mitchell, survived in the port area of Dublin for a good length of time, broadcasting regular weather reports. He arrived with a fair amount of money, in both British and American currencies, and was not shy

Above: Both *U37* and *U38*, which landed agents in Ireland, were large Type IXA boats built at Deschimag AG Weser in Bremen. This probably shows *U43*, an identical type from the same shipyard. They were characterised by an especially wide upper deck as can be seen here.

Right: Although the Type IXA had a comparatively large conning tower, it is highly unlikely that the agents would have been allowed up top for any length of time. At sea, only four lookouts, the duty officer and the commander plus the gun crew had the opportunity of sampling fresh air. In safe areas, one or two smokers might also have been allowed out for a brief period. Although British air cover had been extended to the Western Approaches by the time agents were being landed in Ireland, commanders often did not have the gun crews standing-by next to guns because getting them below added to the diving time. It was often preferred to evade aircraft by diving quickly.

Above: The doctor from the supply U-boat, *U460,* being transferred to *U758* in mid-Atlantic. This shows how difficult it was to paddle inflatables even under good conditions when the weather was warm enough for shorts. Many agents were landed during the winter months when it was necessary to wear several clumsy layers of clothing as well as a life-jacket.

Above: The medical officer of *U178* being transferred to *U509.* These inflatables were pretty good for ferrying people, but their soft rubber floors did not stand up too well to carrying heavy boxes. The bottoms were frequently ripped out once heavy loads were placed inside.

Above: Two men from *U69* rowing their rubber dinghy.

in spending it. For example, rather than quietly taking a train to Dublin, he crossed the country by taxi. It seems likely that he also earned his own living by running a small shop but the exact reason for his eventual discovery appears to have got lost among the piles of documents hidden away from public gaze.

At about the same time as Ernst Weber-Drohl was being landed in Killala Bay, an Irishman called Sean Russell walked into the German consulate in Genoa in Italy to offer his services to Hitler's war effort. It appears that he had been forced to make a hurried exit from the United States because his visa there had expired and the American authorities were not too keen on the manner in which he had been raising money for the IRA among the Irish-American community. No one in Germany could find an immediate use for Russell, but his somewhat audacious lifestyle, his strong IRA background and the fact that he was resourceful enough to reach Germany by crossing the Atlantic as a sailor aboard a neutral ship made him an attractive personality.

Some time before Russell was first interviewed, steps had been taken to extract another Irishman, Frank Ryan, from a Spanish jail. Although he had been on the Republican side during the Spanish Civil War and various people were screaming for his head, he was fortunate enough to have had his death sentence commuted to life imprisonment. It is unclear why the Germans, who had supported Franco's Nationalists, should have been instrumental in orchestrating his escape from jail, but Ryan arrived in Germany, where Russell asked whether he would accompany him on the mission to Ireland.

Both of them had such powerful connections to the IRA that they were not entrusted with any special obligations. Instead the Abwehr was happy to transport them back to their homeland in the hope that they created positive propaganda for Germany. Having such enthusiastic characters based firmly on Irish soil was thought to be a good foundation for future agents who might have to be injected into that country. Had anyone created these two men in a work of fiction, then no doubt many readers would take them to be somewhat far-fetched. They were two highly ingenious individuals, who were both prepared to steer exceedingly close to the wind for their cause. So far their life histories had been bizarre. What was to follow was even more unbelievable and would hardly get past a realistic fiction editor.

The boat chosen to execute Operation *Taube* ('Dove') was *U65* under Hans-Gerrit von Stockhausen, which had been commissioned only some six months earlier, in mid-February 1940. However, von Stockhausen was no newcomer to submarines. He had been one of the first commanders and gained ample experience with *U13* long before the war. Like Werner Hartmann of *U37,* he had also been a flotilla leader.

The plans for dropping off the agents had probably not been finalised by the time *U65* left Wilhelmshaven on 8 August 1940 because von Stockhausen initially took up a position from where he could reach both Ireland and the shipping lanes of the North Atlantic. The order to proceed with the special mission did not come until midday on 13 August. By that time, *U65* was fighting with a number of niggling little problems, the most annoying of which had been an irritating rattle from one of the rescue buoys. Although the installation of these devices was being discontinued, they were still fitted as standard features to a number of boats. Even as the signal from the U-boat Command was coming in, *U65*'s first watch officer and another man climbed into the drenching waves of a force 7-8 southwesterly literally to bash the buoy out of its fitting before cutting the cable with a hacksaw. A short time later, the lid to the buoy's storage container received the same treatment as punishment for

Above: The upper deck of *U1228* with a different type of inflatable dinghy. This variety was designed to carry one man sitting on the right, where the wall was thicker and with his feet towards the left where the rubber ring was thinner. Paddling this type of craft was exceedingly difficult because of the wide barrier between the body and the water. Steering it was even more of a problem and the dinghies tended to drift in whatever direction the wind was blowing.

The other alternative, that of storing the body inside one of the torpedo tubes, was also impractical because they would all be required for the forthcoming foray. Unfortunately, these plans were also jinxed. A few days later, lookouts spotted a noticeable oil slick in their wake, leaving them no alternative other than to make for dry dock in France. Going on into battle trailing such an obvious advert would have been suicidal.

Ryan vanished from the espionage scene to live in Berlin until he died four years later, at the age of 38. Von Stockhausen returned to his role as flotilla commander but also faced an early end in a car accident in Berlin on 15 January 1943. This pair of untimely deaths has given rise to further masses of conjecture. The cheaper and more unscrupulous magazines have floated a variety of explanations from poisoning by the Russian secret service to retribution from IRA agents in Germany, but all of them are without foundation.

Although it seems likely that there were no more landing attempts from U-boats, the Abwehr was also using small yachts for ferrying people to and from Ireland, and aircraft were used for parachute drops. These stories are almost certainly based on fact, but the details have been elaborately embroidered and it is now difficult to establish the dividing line between fact and fiction.

Above: Jak Mallmann, the author's father, using *U377's* wooden dinghy in Norway. These were sturdy little boats but could hardly carry two men and their luggage. The special flotation tanks running along both sides of the boat are clearly visible.

starting its own noisy commotion. While this was going on, the men inside the boat were experiencing another kind of drama centring around Russell who was complaining of severe stomach cramps. The symptoms were a long way beyond the capabilities of the U-boat's paramedic, who had been taught some first aid for injuries, but not the skills to identify and treat internal complaints. Trying out the obvious remedies for constipation did not help and two days later Russell dropped down dead.

Von Stockhausen was prepared to continue with the special mission. However, Ryan had met Russell only a few days earlier and was not really sure what this was supposed to be. What's more, his slight deafness, combined with the need for utter secrecy, had prevented them from discussing details in the noisy U-boat. Not knowing whether he would succeed in finding contacts or friends in Ireland, Ryan decided against landing alone.

The U-boat Command was informed by radio that the operation had been abandoned. Then von Stockhausen ordered the corpse to be sown into bedsheets for a military funeral at sea. He was going on, to participate in the convoy battles, and it could be several weeks before he reached port, so this was a case of wanting to dispose of the body for hygiene reasons, rather than leaving Russell in the waters close to his homeland.

Above: Men of *U200* struggling with a different type of dinghy. It was stored upside-down under the planking below the men's feet when not in use. Plug holes in the bottom were opened to allow the air out and the boat to fill with water when the submarine dived.

Left: This photograph, taken from *U461* (one of the submarine supply tankers), shows that wooden U-boat dinghies were no cheap rowing boats but carefully constructed craft which would not sink, even when filled with water. This made them well suited for the difficult conditions submarines were likely to encounter.

Left: The frozen salty waters of the Jade estuary during the winter of 1940 when *U37* had to cross this barrier before reaching the open waters of the North Sea to carry an agent to Ireland.

Above: Korvkpt Hans-Gerrit von Stockhausen on the conning tower of *U65* with four lookouts and the duty officer. The commander's flagpole can be seen to the right in front of the single 20mm anti-aircraft gun.

Above: U65, a long-range Type IXB during August 1940, shortly after having put in to Brest to repair the oil leak which caused Korvkpt Stockhausen to break off the mission after the agent Sean Russell died on board from natural causes. The boat originally put in to Lorient to join the 2nd U-Flotilla (Flotilla Saltzwedel), but a shortage of dry dock facilities there made it necessary to move further north to Brest. Since the camera can see through the camouflage netting rather well, one wonders whether this was of any use against aircraft. The net cutter on the bows is a leftover feature from earlier times.

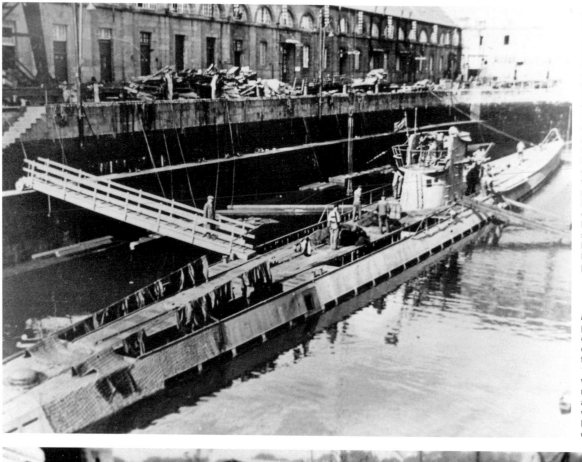

Left: Another view of *U65* in the same dry dock which has now been flooded. It is difficult to determine whether this photograph was taken at the beginning or end of the overhaul, although the untidy deck, with blankets drying on the jumping wires, would suggest that the boat has recently come from a hectic period at sea, rather than having spent the last few days in port.

Below: This photograph of *U65* was taken during the first three months of 1941, while she was being repaired in Lorient after an eventful voyage to the Freetown area of Africa.

Right: Killala Post Office as it is now, over fifty years after Ernst Weber-Drohl landed there from *U37*.

Below: The idyllic desolation of Killala Bay in Ireland, close to the spot where the ex-strongman, Ernst Weber-Drohl, landed from *U37*.

Chapter 2
Icelandic Betrayals and Failures

The first wartime U-boat landing in Iceland worked exceptionally well, but all subsequent attempts resulted in failure or betrayal and in unfortunate consequences for the boats. Only one boat returned after landing agents to provide an account of what had happened. The other three were lost a few days after the completion of their special mission.

That first landing took place a few days after the beginning of the war, when *U30* under Kptlt Fritz-Julius Lemp brought an injured crewman to the German consul in Reykjavik, Professor Gerlach, who was also a well-known surgeon. *U30*, famous for sinking the liner *Athenia* on the first day of the war, had sent a boarding party to the freighter *Fanad Head* when three aircraft from HMS *Ark Royal* attacked. Two of them were brought down by explosions from their own bombs while the U-boat was hardly damaged, but the situation was made more confusing by the injured Matrosenobergefreiter Otto Ohse jumping overboard to rescue one of the airmen. To make matters even worse, the boarding party was still aboard the freighter, setting scuttling charges. Having retrieved his crew and taken care of two surviving airmen, Lemp was faced with the unenviable task of either having to watch Maschinenmaat Adolf Schmidt die from the loss of blood through shrapnel wounds or get him to a hospital, hence the unorthodox step of asking permission to land in neutral Iceland.

U30 slipped into the harbour of Reykjavik at 10 o'clock in the morning on 19 September 1939. The incident has been documented in the journal *Das Archiv* and by the journal *The U-boat Archive* as follows:

'The German consul, Dr Gerlach, a doctor of medicine, went on board to treat the wounded, while Maschinenmaat Adolf Schmidt was taken over to the German freighter Hamm by an Icelandic customs boat and later transferred to the hospital (St Josefs-Spital) in town. After this, U30 took on board bread and other provisions from German ships lying at anchor in the harbour. This included a turkey with the name "Alfons" who lived throughout the voyage in the electro-motor room and created considerable excitement when the boat arrived in Wilhelmshaven with him secured to the boat's gun. The 3rd Officer of the freighter Hamm was transferred on board U30 as replacement for Schmidt and then U30 departed again at about 14.00 hours. The two British pilots became prisoners of war in Germany until 1945.*

'On 20 September 1939, the Icelandic newspaper Morgunbladid published a photograph of Adolf Schmidt stepping from the customs launch with his arm in bandages. He became patient number 950 of 1939 at St Josefs-Spital in Reykjavik. His address on the admittance form is given as "Wilhelmshaven, U30, Salzwedel Flotilla". [Note that the correct spelling should be Saltzwedel.] He remained in care for 33 days and then lived for a short while in Hotel Island before being offered quarters with a Germany family. He promised not to attempt an escape and was therefore free to move about the town. In May 1940 the German consul warned him of the imminent Allied occupation, as a result of which he succeeded in hiding for*

a few days before being captured on the 23rd and subsequently brought to Liverpool. From there he was transferred to Canada, where he met a number of his former shipmates from U30 in the prison camp.'

The first agent of the planned Icelandic spy network had no intention of working for Germany. It seems instead that he used the opportunity of becoming an agent to beat the absence of civilian transport and return to his homeland. When he was landed from *U252* on 6 April 1942 Ib Riis made a beeline for the comfort of the nearest farm and gave himself up. Officialdom was far enough away for him to remain there for the best part of a week before the police arrived to arrest him. Even once Riis had reached the nearest village, he still had to mark time for several days before transport to Reykjavik could be organised and it was the end of the month before he was in the hands of the British war machine. Following intensive interrogation in Scotland, he was eventually returned to Iceland to set up his transmitter under Royal Navy supervision so that he could broadcast whatever snippets of disinformation Allied intelligence gave him.

The second agent, Jens Fridriksson who landed from *U279* on 20 September 1943, suffered a similar fate, although he did not give himself up. He was captured before establishing himself in the Icelandic capital. Life was then made uncomfortable until he had no choice other than to obey the wishes of his new masters. He, too, broadcast messages for Allied intelligence.

The third landing brought two men ashore from *U289* on 25 April 1944, but both Sverrir Matthiasson and Magnus Gudbjörnsson were arrested shortly afterwards. The Allied authorities obviously had no use for another set of puppets and instructed Riis to broadcast news of their arrest. Before that could be done, another espionage team was landed by *U955* on 30 April 1944. This time the three men, Ernst Fresenius, Sigurdur Juliusson and Hjalti Björnsson were pinned down on the coast by an intense snowstorm. Remaining in a small cave without the necessary survival gear, they ran short of food and would have given themselves up, had Fresenius's strong sympathies for Germany and his pistol not prevented the other two from throwing in the towel. The trio did not remain free for long. By the end of their second week in Iceland they were all in Allied custody.

It would seem with most of these agents that the Abwehr made the fundamental mistake of training Icelanders who were more keen on finding a way of crossing the dangerous Atlantic to reach their homeland than supporting the German war effort. The others, who were prepared to spy for Germany, were too inexperienced to survive for any length of time and this deficiency also applied to the U-boat commanders.

U252 was commissioned on 4 October 1941, just six months before the Icelandic landing, by Kptlt Günter Schiebusch, who was taken ill shortly afterwards and remained in hospital until the following March. His replacement, Kptlt Kai Lerchen, had been born aboard a ship on its way from South Africa to Germany with a stop-over in England and hence his birth was

Above: U30 running into Wilhelmshaven after having landed an injured man in Iceland. The emblem of the dog, painted by the radio operator Georg Högel a few days after the beginning of the war, was probably the first insignia ever to appear on a U-boat conning tower. Note the early conning tower design with the upward-curving wind deflector along the top edge.

officially registered in London. He started his U-boat training after a brief spell as artillery officer of the heavy cruiser *Admiral Hipper*, and then spent a couple of months aboard *U85* as watch officer. Following this, Lerchen attended U-boat commanders' school for just one month before being thrown into action with *U252*. Four months later he and his crew were dead.

Kptlt Otto Finke of *U279* joined the navy in 1936, three years after Lerchen, having come home to the Reich from the Far East. He was born in Sumatra and had established himself as a minesweeping squadron commander when he asked to step sideways to join the 3rd U-boat Flotilla for general submarine training. This was just as inadequate as that received by Lerchen, but Finke survived for a few months longer before he and his crew were sunk.

The third of the trio to be lost shortly after landing agents in Iceland was Oberleutnant-zur-See (ObltzS) Hans-Heinrich Baden, who commissioned *U955* at the end of 1942, though it was a year before the boat sailed for its first operational mission. Baden had previously been watch officer aboard *U558* for 12 months which made him quite experienced by the standards applied during the war, when the majority of men were sent out with very little training. However, he did not wear the white commander's cap for long. *U955* went down before returning from her first mission.

Kptlt Alexander Hellwig of *U289* was lucky to return from his mission to land agents in Iceland, but his boat went down during the following voyage, killing all 51 men on board.

U252's special mission in April 1942 coincided with rather a turbulent period. The United States had joined in the war just four months earlier and most eyes were still firmly focused on America, though the British attack on St Nazaire on 27 March had become a talking point on the European side of the big

pond. Kptlt Lerchen put in to Heligoland in *U252* on the morning after the attack on St Nazaire, but not to commiserate about Germany's losses. Following a few minor repairs, he continued his journey with the knowledge that he was far away from any known hotspot. We know that the landing in Iceland was successful because, as we have seen, Ib Riis certainly got ashore and the absence of any radio reports suggests that *U252* had an uneventful voyage.

The boat's first attack, two days later, was also successful. Possibly this was a result of vigilance being relaxed around the convoys because the U-boats had been concentrating on the eastern seaboard of the United States. Whatever, *U252* torpedoed a small freighter, the SS *Fanefield*, which had just emerged from the shelter of the rugged Icelandic coastline. This may have lulled Lerchen and his men into a false sense of security but four days later they were sunk by escorts from convoy OG.82, victims of the famous Captain (Capt) F. J. Walker in HMS *Stork* who on this occasion was hunting with Lieutenant-Commander (Lt-Cdr) K. M. B. Menzies in HMS *Vetch*. The U-boat Command had no idea what had happened. Following his report of the convoy, Lerchen was told he could attack whenever it suited him because there were no other boats in the vicinity and he was informed that he could not expect any support. However, he was warned not to remain with a convoy during the hours of daylight. Aircraft flying from bases in Iceland had been making too much of an impression in recent months.

The following day, when Lerchen failed to respond to a signal requesting his position, Dönitz became concerned. It was assumed that he had suffered a similar fate to *U82* (Kptlt Siegfried Rollmann), which had been lost in the area two months earlier. Dönitz thought that the Allies could be sailing specially well-protected groups of merchant ships for the sole purpose of hunting U-boats. Therefore he prohibited all attacks against convoys in the Icelandic area. Such convoys never existed, and Lerchen's loss can be blamed on the combination of an inexperienced crew and well-trained escorts.

U279 sailed into one of the worst U-boat disasters of World War 2, the catastrophe of the Rossbach Pack, but survived to be sunk some time later as a result of patient persistence by an American pilot with the Germanic name of Westhofen. He first sighted *U279* on the surface close to Iceland, but could not get his Ventura bomber close enough for an attack. Commander (Cdr) C. L. Westhofen and his crew returned to the spot some two hours later but found empty seas. However, they had plenty of fuel because they had flown from Iceland, not from the far-off shores of Europe or America and were able to keep hunting. Returning for a third time to the area where the U-boat had dived, they were fortunate enough to spot their quarry on the surface. The sun was behind their aircraft as it screeched down at top speed with guns blazing while the navigator concentrated on the right moment to release the set of depth charges. Despite being in such an unfortunate position, the gunners on *U279* were alert and the last stages of the attack were carried out through a barrage of intense anti-aircraft fire, catching Westhofen by surprise. *U279* was one of the first U-boats to be fitted with the increased anti-aircraft armament. Some eight large barrels plus a few smaller machine guns put up an impressive and effective burst of fire but three

depth charges crashed down within 15m of the boat and wrecked it beyond further use. Trailing smoke and hardly capable of gaining height, the Ventura could not even report the sinking nor summon help for the U-boat men struggling with life-rafts because their radio had been put out of action. Yet, with such a large number of men on the deck to work the guns, many of them managed to jump into the sea, but it was October and the waters around Iceland were already extremely cold. None of them reached land.

U955 was also one of the many to fall foul of a determined pilot. Having left Kiel on 23 March 1944, the boat put in to Kristiansand (Norway) for minor repairs before heading out towards Iceland. It was *U955's* first voyage and the appearance of niggling faults, requiring dockyard facilities to put right, had become a feature of German submarine production. The landing of the agents in Iceland then took place uneventfully but a few days later *U955* was detected close to the northwest tip of Spain, on the way home via the Bay of Biscay. The submarine shot down one aircraft but was then sunk by a Sunderland, piloted by Flying Officer L. Baveystock, on 6 June 1944. There were no survivors.

U252, the fourth boat involved with landings in Iceland, put in to Narvik (northern Norway) after the successful conclusion of the mission, having been at sea for a brief period of just over two weeks. Following this, she went out towards the loneliness of Jan Mayen, where she was sunk by the destroyer HMS *Milne* under Capt M. Richmond.

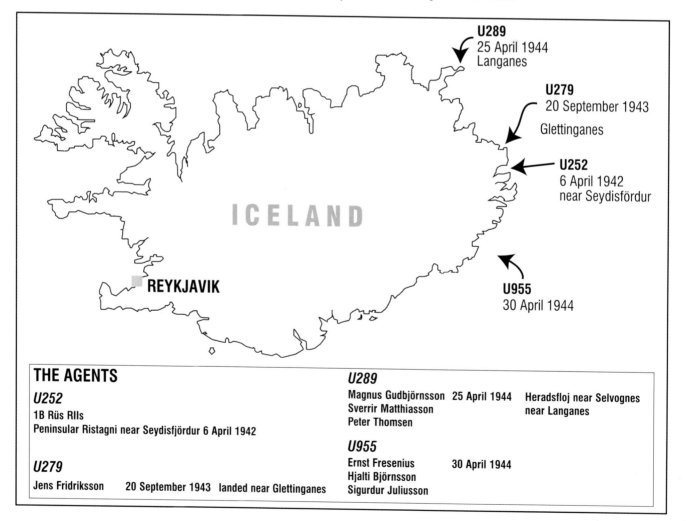

THE AGENTS

U252
1B Rüs RIIs
Peninsular Ristagni near Seydisfjördur 6 April 1942

U279
Jens Fridriksson   20 September 1943   landed near Glettinganes

U289

Magnus Gudbjörnsson	25 April 1944	Heradsfloj near Selvognes
Sverrir Matthiasson		near Langanes
Peter Thomsen		

U955

Ernst Fresenius	30 April 1944
Hjalti Björnsson	
Sigurdur Juliusson	

Left: The boats used to land agents in Iceland were of the smaller Type VIIC variety. This shows *U755* (Kptlt Walter Göing) around the time it was operating against convoys along the Algerian, Tunisian and Moroccan coasts. The camouflage pattern painted on the side featured on several Mediterranean boats and was probably not used in the Atlantic, but apart from that, *U755* looked identical to the submarines used to land agents in Iceland. One of the typical features was the long and narrow upper deck. Note that the net cutter no longer features on the bows. The wire running up from the tow-hole at the front to the top of the conning tower served as a radio aerial and also as an anchorage for safety harnesses when men worked out in the open during rough weather.

Right: The bows of *U755* while refuelling at sea, showing how cramped and difficult it was when a large number of men had to work on the upper deck. It is possible to distinguish the bows from the stern by the single jumping wire running from the top of the conning tower to the front. On the stern there were usually two. This rule of thumb worked for most of the war, except for a brief period towards the end of 1942 and the beginning of 1943 when rigid radar aerials were fixed to a few conning towers.

Chapter 3
Sabotage in the United States

To prevent an escalation of hostilities at the beginning of World War 2, German Military Intelligence was prohibited from spying in the United States. Therefore, two years later, when Hitler declared war on America, his espionage departments had to start with clean sheets to lay meaningful foundations among the comparatively large but diffuse German communities in the new world. A hurried evaluation of the problems and opportunities revealed that spying was going to be considerably less attractive than sabotage operations. It was assumed that sufficient German sympathisers could be found to supply the information necessary for striking vital blows at the industrial back-up for the American war machine. What was needed were leaders to organise this potential force into effective resistance and to teach volunteers worthwhile sabotage techniques. The number of Germans in the United States was quite considerable, many having emigrated earlier in the century.

While sabotage plans were being formulated, promising potential agents underwent training for a variety of destructive undertakings. Unfortunately, despite the Nazis having created what has often appeared as a highly effective secret police, the Gestapo, the selection of agents seems to have been left to incompetent amateurs who had little or no knowledge of the difficulties which these men were going to face. There were cases of agents being landed who could not speak the local language and one in which two men were expected to carry their gear, including a heavy radio with electricity generator, for several hundred kilometres through the Namibian desert.

In addition to such obvious shortcomings, the clandestine German thrust against the United States also disregarded a number of basic espionage rules. Security procedures for activation when one member of the team was captured were not devised, and instead each agent knew enough about everybody else to throw the entire project into jeopardy if he passed his knowledge on to the enemy. However, the navy was not aware of these defects when Dönitz was ordered to ferry the men across the Atlantic.

Two boats, *U202* and *U584*, were chosen for the ambitious project of infiltrating the first team of eight saboteurs into the United States. *U202* under Kptlt Hans-Heinz Linder was well qualified for the job. He had commissioned the boat over a year earlier, in March 1941, and then led three successful voyages to the southern Greenland area of the North Atlantic. Following this, *U202* joined Operation *Paukenschlag* ('Drum Roll'), the initial attack on the United States. This was quite remarkable because *U202* was not one of the large 'ocean-going' types, but a standard Type VIIC, without additional fuel bunkers. Attempts to send such boats across the Atlantic proved far more successful than had been anticipated and showed that Type VII boats could cover considerably longer distances than experts had calculated.

Operation *Paukenschlag* worked exceedingly well and the small boats reaped an impressive harvest along the eastern seaboard of the United States, although the U-boat Command did take a considerable risk. Previously it had been the policy to refuel boats before the start of aggressive action, to ensure that they had a sufficient supply to return home independently without having to use the radio. This time boats were refuelled after the action which meant that the opposition had some idea of where they might still be. Therefore the U-boat Command provided opportunities for them to be pursued by superior forces which could easily destroy both U-boat and supplier at a most vulnerable period of time. The reason for not doing it the other way round was that the plans were conceived in such a hurry that there was not enough time to dispatch the large supply boats ahead of the fighting submarines.

U202 almost did not make it as far as American waters and could have ended her days as a member of the Mediterranean flotillas, had it not been for a persistent Swordfish from 812 Squadron of the Fleet Air Arm which prevented the boat from making it through the narrows between Gibraltar and North Africa. The damage forced the *U202* back to Brest. Following repairs, *U202* took part in that first thrust against the United States, before taking on board a group of four 'shipyard workers' and a number of heavy packages. Some half-hearted attempts were made to explain the presence of civilians by spreading the word that *U202* was about to participate in trials of a new weapon. It was only after the boat had cleared the dangerous Bay of Biscay that the crew was told about the true nature of their special mission, to land the four in a sandy bay near Amagansett on Long Island, a short distance east of New York.

The voyage was uneventful until *U202* was far enough across the Atlantic to make a turnaround impractical. At that stage, Obergefreiter Zimmermann, one of the torpedo mechanics, started complaining of stomach pains. He was not the type to dodge duties and his discomfort was quickly emphasised by a rapid increase in temperature. There was very little anyone could do to help. *U202* did not have a doctor and the need to maintain radio silence meant that Linder could not ask for help either. Zimmermann could only be supplied with cold compresses and opium to make the pain of a suspected appendicitis bearable. In fact the boat's entire stock of opium was consumed and later morphine had to be used to keep his groans in the cramped quarters bearable.

U202 had left Brest on 27 May 1942 and had been at sea for 16 days by the time the landing procedure started. The idea was to approach the sandy beach with the boat surfaced but trimmed low in the water, so low that it would only just be possible to walk on the upper deck without getting wet. This had the advantage of showing a small silhouette and, at the same time, made it possible to reduce the draft and lift the boat a good couple of metres higher in an emergency. Linder was planning to go in very slowly, nose first, until the boat touched land. Then his men would help the agents ashore and the U-boat would go astern and move back out to sea. It was a sensible plan, but as has often been the case, nature provided some good opportunities for a chain of infuriating cock-ups.

The first of these occurred early during the final run-in, which Linder had ordered to be made underwater. The idea was to remain undetected until a water depth of 20m under the submerged keel had been reached, but the boat had not gone very far when an unexpected shudder told everybody that they had just hit the first part of the American continent. Linder

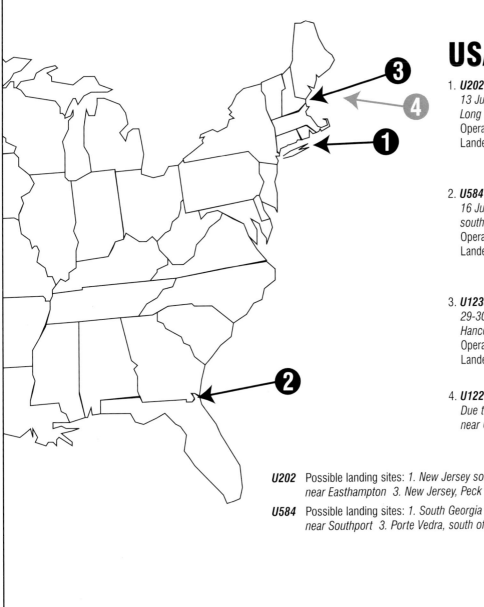

USA Landings

1. **U202** Kptlt. Hans-Heinz Linder
   *13 June 1942, landed at Amagansett,
   Long Island*
   Operation: *Pastorius*
   Landed: *Ernst Burger, Geaorge Dasch
                   Heinrich Heinck & Richard
                   Quirin*

2. **U584** Kptlt. Joachim Deecke
   *16 June 1942, landed near Ponte Vedra,
   south of Jacksonville in Florida*
   Operation: *Pastorius*
   Landed: *Herbert Haupt, Edward
                   Kerling, Hermann Neubauer &
                   Werner Thiel*

3. **U1230** Kptlt. Hans Hilbig
   *29-30 November 1944, landed at
   Hancock Point in Frenchman's Bay*
   Operation: *Elster*
   Landed: *Erich Gimpel & William Curtis
                   Colepaugh*

4. **U1229** Korvkpt. Armin Zinke
   *Due to land agent Oskar Mantel in or
   near Gulf of Maine but sank en-route*

U202   Possible landing sites: *1. New Jersey south of Seaside Park 2. Long Island near Easthampton 3. New Jersey, Peck Beach by Ocean City*

U584   Possible landing sites: *1. South Georgia near Jacksonville 2. North Carolina near Southport 3. Porte Vedra, south of Jacksonville, Florida*

carefully worked the boat free and surfaced to find himself surrounded by an impenetrable pea-soup fog. Visibility was absolutely nil, which, in a way, was ideal for clandestine activities. *U202* continued creeping extremely slowly towards the sandy beach using the silent electric motors. Another violent jerk assured that there was no mistaking the arrival and then, at about six o'clock in the morning, the well-discussed landing procedure was given the go-ahead.

A large inflatable raft was already lying ready on the foredeck, together with a long line of rope to make sure it could not become fully detached from the submarine. Dönitz had heard about the earlier chaotic experiences with Luftwaffe dinghies and this time provided the men with a decent raft, which was less likely to be turned over by surf. Everything went well, although the landing took a little longer than anticipated because the boat had not come to a halt on the beach, but on a sandbank some 200m out in a moderate surf.

Unable to see anything because of the fog, the lookouts strained their ears for clues as to what was happening. They heard very little, other than waves washing on the beach. This meant that it took a while to discover that the swell had swung the boat round so that it was now lying parallel to the shore, rather than with just the bows touching the sand. Linder, however, had taken the precaution of having planned a head-checking system, making a delay for a roll-call unnecessary before he ordered the departure.

Unfortunately, the motors did not detach *U202* from America's firm hold. Linder reacted quickly. Instantly he ordered the tanks to be flooded again to prevent the boat being washed further onto what he thought was the beach. It was going to take a few precious minutes to start the diesel engines and clutch them onto the shafts. Then the tanks were blown once more for another, considerably more powerful, attempt to pull free. Strong vibrations produced a dramatic foaming effect along both sides and water blown under the hull by the propellers running full astern temporarily rocked the boat but there was no significant movement. To make matters worse, the fog started to lift. It also appeared as if the noise from the diesels had caused a dog to bark in the distance. When a machine gun opened fire and searchlights from the nearby radio station flooded over the bay, the men in U202 wondered whether they had been discovered, but both these intrusive irritations were too far away to be a direct threat. It was a Wednesday morning. Cars were now just about visible on a nearby road, taking their passengers on their way to work. The crew could only hope that people did not have time or inclination to peer into the water and those who might hear the diesel engines would think the noise was from an aircraft. As long as the fog persisted there was little danger of anyone seeing the boat clearly, but Linder did spare a thought for the four agents, hoping that the dog would not be too inquisitive and annoy them by drawing in human back-up.

The next frantic attempt to pull free made it quite clear that there was no longer sufficient water under the hull to float the boat. What was more, an ebbing tide ensured that the submarine remained firmly lodged on the beach like a stranded whale, slowly listing until it settled at an angle of 40°. This made movement not only uncomfortable but incredibly difficult and meant men started walking on the walls like flies. Despite the precarious predicament, Linder remained cool. Vital pieces of machinery already had scuttling charges attached and now was the time to prepare the interior for total destruction. At the same time the men got ready for quick disembarkation, while the radio operator coded a message for U202's final transmission to headquarters. Linder did not beat about the bush. He told his men that they would try everything to get free, but they might as well adjust their minds to becoming prisoners of war. He ordered Oberbootmannsmaat Mühlhausen to bring the by now seriously ill Zimmermann ashore and to remain with him. There was no way that he could be moved quickly and Linder was not going to leave him behind. The end of his command looked infuriatingly close and rather than save his boat, he was now looking for ways of making his men's future as secure as possible.

Although the fog was clearing and the shadow of the shore could be made out, no one on land seemed interested in the boat's presence. Two unimaginably long hours of high tension passed without interference before lookouts reported the first signs of the incoming tide. It was nine o'clock by the time Linder could make another desperate attempt to detach U202 from the firm American grip. Using their last air for maximum lift, Linder and the engineering officer tried something they had never done before. It was one of those tricks they had heard about, but the majority of men never got into such a predicament that they had to use it. This was to apply every ounce of available power by connecting both the diesel engines and the electric motors to the propeller shafts. Doing this, they managed to achieve what the engineering officer thought was an impossibly high number of revolutions. The rudder was then jerked quickly from side to side, inducing a fierce swinging action which eventually helped to wriggle the boat free.

Despite an indescribable feeling of elation, the cheer of relief came under the men's breath because they did not want to draw attention to themselves. Although the land could now be made out quite clearly, meaning that observers would also be able to spot the boat, it was still too foggy to see Zimmermann and Mühlhausen ashore. Someone had to go out to retrieve the two before U202 headed out to sea. Compressors were running at maximum to replenish the air supplies and, as soon as practical, the boat disappeared below the waves. Linder thought that his men had had enough excitement for one night and he would give them the opportunity of a good rest before asking them to exert themselves again. Despite the chaotic experience and very nearly ending up paraded through New York, morale was good. No one seemed to blame the old man for the rather nasty predicament.

It was another two days before Linder was confident of being far enough away to risk a radio call saying that the mission had been successfully accomplished and, at the same time, he asked for advice about what to do with Zimmermann. Strangely, Zimmermann had started showing signs of recovery by the time the reply rolled in and morale aboard U202 was boosted even further by the sinking of two ships. First was the 4860-ton Argentinian freighter *Rio Tercero* nine days after the landing and then the 5861-ton American freighter *City of Birmingham* on 1 July 1942. Ten days after this U202 was refuelled from U460 under command of Kptlt Friedrich Schäfer, one of the 10 purpose-built supply submarines, the first of which had entered service only a short time before this most welcome meeting.

The other half of this operation, that of landing four men near Jacksonville in Florida by U584 under Kptlt Joachim Deecke, went considerably more smoothly than U202's nerve-tingling adventure. It is an unusual coincidence that the same first watch officer, Hermann Lamby, had served in both these U-boats. He had had the good fortune of having left U754 (Hans Oestermann) a few days before that boat set out for its last voyage, from which there were no survivors. He was then appointed to the post of first watch officer in U202, but was moved to U584 before having had the opportunity of sailing with Linder. Later, a few days before Christmas 1942, Lamby moved on once more to become commander of U437 and in February 1945 he took on U3029, one of the new and revolutionary Type XXI boats.

U584 left Brest on 25 May 1942 and for Lamby and the rest of the crew the crossing of the Atlantic was relatively easy, with only the restless sea and uncooperative weather adding any discomfort to the proceedings, though the voyage was not too rough. Orders for both U202 and U584 stated that commanders were free to engage in offensive action if suitable targets presented themselves, but nothing crossed their paths, meaning it was a more than usually monotonous 22 days before U584 reached its destination. Lamby and one other man, whose name he has forgotten, rowed the four agents Herbert Haupt, Hermann Neubauer, Werner Thiel and their leader, Edward Kerling, ashore. Lamby filled his empty bailing tin with American sand and sent a recognition signal with his torch to the boat, which he could hardly make out. Then both men paddled back to disappear into the blackness from which they had come. It was a pleasant, calm night, so warm that the men heard giggling night-time female bathers, so that the outing was rather a refreshing undertaking. Once they were safely back on board, U584 sailed northwards and succeeded in sinking a ship before a shortage of fuel forced it eastwards to meet U460, the same supply U-boat which refuelled U202.

The agents carried by U584 disappeared into Jacksonville without too many difficulties. The other group, landed by U202, consisting of Ernst Burger, Heinrich Heinck, Richard Quirin and the leader George Dasch, were faced with considerable problems which almost prevented them from getting off the beach. Long before the United States joined in the war, American warmongers had already instilled a deep-seated fear into the population and once the weapons were unleashed, the media made the feeble-minded think that Germany might attempt an invasion of the eastern seaboard. The hate generated against Hitler's war machine had put the entire population on alert and probably also discouraged possible sabotage activities by German sympathisers, many of whom had become recognised citizens of the United States. This frenzied imagination, whipped up by lively propaganda, reached as far as keeping an army of people occupied for checking deserted shores. One of these lone patrolmen stumbled upon the four agents landed by *U202*.

John Cullen, whose torch light was seen from *U202*, had a fistful of dollars thrust at him and was told to keep quiet about this illicit 'fishing party'. This might have worked, but he was then threatened with his life before being released to stagger back up the beach. Although Cullen's reinforcements discovered the packages buried by the four Germans, the agents vanished into New York. They could, no doubt, have remained free for a long time, had it not been for Dasch giving himself up and revealing all he knew to the authorities. Consequently the rest of the group were quickly captured and brought to trial. Two of them were executed. Dasch had also known about the group landed by *U584* and disclosed enough information to enable them too to be arrested. They were tried by special court and sentenced to death by electric chair. Only Dasch and Burger survived to be repatriated to Germany after the war.

One wonders whether they could ever have succeeded in establishing a useful network of saboteurs. The men's training had been quite extensive, but much of it sounds as if it had come from a Tony Hancock or Dad's Army script and included placing sand into vital parts of locomotives, putting aluminium smelters out of action by breaking their power supply and making explosives with substances easily purchased from chemists. Even if the group had remained at large, it seems highly unlikely that such a band could have recruited sufficient numbers to inflict any significant wounds on the might of the United States.

Below: U466, a Type VIIC with a modified conning tower similar to that on U202 which KptLt Linder took across the Atlantic. The large 88mm deck gun has been removed and an additional platform for an anti-aircraft gun has been added at the rear. However, it appears that the original Wintergarten has not yet been enlarged and still accommodates a single 20mm anti-aircraft gun.

Chapter 4
Investigating American Atom Bombs and Jet Aircraft

During the summer of 1944 the possibility of Allied atom bombs and jet aircraft being developed threw the decision-making machinery of the German High Command into turmoil. Research had suggested that a single atomic bomb could probably destroy an entire city and as yet there was no defence against the new jet aircraft already entering service with Germany's own Luftwaffe. Since there was little concrete knowledge of Allied developments, only a great deal of conjecture, the high command proposed to infiltrate spies to determine the level of progress in the United States.

Once again the Abwehr produced a list of somewhat dubious agents. The man chosen as leader, Erich Gimpel, spoke English so badly that he would have made a bus conductor or an official in a railway ticket office suspicious. It is difficult to imagine how he was going to impersonate a military officer, something which he might have to do if he was going to gain access to the information which he was supposed to be seeking. One of his two colleagues, William Curtis Colepaugh, was described as somewhat subnormal by the U-boat crew which ferried him across. To make things even more difficult, both these men were known to have FBI (Federal Bureau of Investigation) records due to earlier subversive activities. The third, independent, member of this group of supposedly technical specialists, Oskar Mantel, had been a bar tender and ladies' hairdresser before the war. He spoke excellent English with the appropriate American accent, but one wonders whether his self-styled importance had also given him the scientific background for understanding the technicalities of his mission.

The planning for infiltrating these men into highly secret American circles was put into operation after the D-Day landings in Normandy, at a time when travel through France was becoming increasingly precarious and submarine missions were difficult to launch from the Biscay ports. In fact, the second boat of this wave to take spies across to America left Germany at about the same time as the last U-boat made its desperate escape from France. In view of this deteriorating situation, both spy-carrying boats were prepared in Kiel, which added not only a considerable distance to their journey, but also involved substantial additional risk of passing more minefields and Allied air patrols.

The two boats selected for these missions were U1229 and U1230. The first mentioned left Kiel on 13 July 1944 under Korvkpt (Korvettenkapitän) Armin Zinke with the agent Oskar Mantel aboard. Unlike the boats used for the earlier missions, this was a large 'ocean-going' Type IXC40, which meant that it had been built with the latest modifications to meet the hazards of the Atlantic. Zinke had commanded minesweepers, the 3rd Minesweeper Flotilla, the Fleet Escort Ship *F5* and then been an instructor at the Barrier School which taught the basics for laying mines before U1229 became his first submarine command. He commissioned the boat in January 1944 and this special undertaking to America, only six months later, was also his first war voyage — and with a 'green' crew. In addition to his obvious lack of experience, Allied interrogation records

later described him as having been a somewhat inept commander, who did much to ruin the morale of his men.

Although U1229 succeeded in crossing the Atlantic safely, the boat was sunk in the gulf off Maine shortly before landing the agent. This came about as a result of one of those quirks, which often proved so fatal in times of war, and started with another U-boat, U802 under Kptlt Helmut Schmoeckel, which was totally unconnected with this operation. U802 was spotted and attacked on the surface by an Avenger aircraft but succeeded in shooting the attacker down. However, all this happened less than 40 miles north of the carrier USS *Bogue*, the Avenger's parent ship. The loss spurred the Americans into an intensive hunt for revenge and they launched another attack, despite the unfavourable weather. A short while later U802 was detected but Schmoeckel was no newcomer to precarious situations and his men successfully used their radar detector to dodge the onslaught. Then, escaping northwards, they continued their activities in the St Lawrence estuary.

Today it is difficult to judge how much Zinke in U1229 knew about these incidents. It was common practice for U-boats to transmit any waiting messages as soon as their position had become known, which would suggest that U-boat Command would have been told about the attack on U802, though destroying the first aircraft may have given Schmoeckel the hope that his position had not been compromised. Whatever may be the truth, the men of the *Bogue* were still on full alert when U802 escaped and U1229 stumbled into their operations area.

U1229 was spotted on the radar screen of an Avenger aircraft and to the pilot's surprise remained on the surface to shoot it out. Near misses from well-placed depth charges resulted in the boat trailing a highly visible oil slick, which then sealed Zinke's fate. Yet, this final battle did not pass without drama. Two attacking Avengers did not notice each other's presence until shortly before they were ready to release their depth charges. Consequently, the pilots concentrated on avoiding each other and the detonations were wide of their target. One of the pilots, though, coolly turned in a huge loop and attacked a second time with a salvo of rockets. These caused the U-boat crew to spill out of the conning tower and launch inflatable dinghies, carried in water- and pressure-resistant containers below the upper deck. Zinke and 17 men died, but the rest, including the agent Oskar Mantel, survived.

After the war there was rather an ironic follow-up. Mantel's family tried suing the commanding officer of *Bogue*, Capt A. B. Vosseller, for the almost $2,000 which Mantel was carrying and had lost, saying that the money had belonged to the family rather than to the German state. One wonders why Mantel had taken the trouble to stuff a bundle of banknotes into his pockets shortly before the sinking? But it could well have been that he had no idea about what was happening, nor his location, and he might have thought that he was in close proximity to the coast. Agents' ignorance of navigational technicalities seems to have been widespread. For example,

Robby Leibbrandt who was brought to South Africa by the sailing yacht *Kyloe*, could not be made to understand that it was necessary to follow the North-East Trade Winds across the Atlantic as far as South America and then cross back over the Atlantic once more by following the Westerlies. He even proved his ignorance by steering into the windless Doldrums. Mantel might well have had the illusion that there was some hope of reaching land undetected.

U1230, under Kptlt Hans Hilbig, left Kiel on 26 October 1944 rather hurriedly to avoid an air raid and anchored in relatively deep water on the shore near the Naval Memorial at Laboe to await two other boats and a minesweeper escort for the passage northwards to Norway. Mines that had escaped from German protective fields and 'wild ones' deposited in the gaps by the Allies had already become a major headache in the western Baltic and in North Sea coastal waters, making movements without escorts highly risky undertakings. *U1230*, also a large ocean-going Type IXC40, was kitted out for a long voyage of at least six months because it was now certain that it could not return to a French Atlantic port. The Allied armies were spreading rapidly through Europe, cutting off the French bases. Officially there was talk of regaining the offensive and pushing the enemy away from those vital ports, but deep-down the men knew that this was just another one of those pipe dreams put about by the propaganda system.

It took a good while before *U1230* was clear of Norwegian minefields and could settle down to cruising submerged during the hours of daylight and making progress with the aid of a schnorkel at night. The fact that a vast number of boats suffered from faulty ventilation systems had hardly been publicised and it looks as if the men in *U1230* were left to their own devices to discover these disadvantages for themselves. The sad point about this problem was that the men often lacked sleep and could not determine the difference between carbon monoxide poisoning and feeling tired. *U1230* was lucky inasmuch that the poisonous fumes filling their boat were accompanied by a good concentration of choking exhaust smoke, forcing the men to reach for their personal Dräger lungs, which doubled up as respirators. They were also lucky that they could surface under a magnificently clear full moon to ventilate the interior without interference from the enemy. It had been essential to leave Norway during the full moon in order to reach the destination at the time of the new moon.

The agent Erich Gimpel fitted very well into the daily life of the U-boat. He made a determined effort to work his passage by participating in the usual watch-keeping duties and helping with kitchen chores. When the echo-sounder broke down, he even had the chance of demonstrating his technical abilities by repairing the complicated apparatus. The U-boat men were impressed by his performance. Many of them lost their inhibitions of having passengers on board and discussed technical submarine matters with this enthusiastic and likeable character. The same cannot be said of his partner, William Colepaugh, who spoke virtually no German and behaved in such a questionable manner that Gimpel exchanged stern words with him at times.

Hans Hilbig, the commander of *U1230*, had joined the navy in 1936, the year of the Olympic Games in Berlin, and had been seconded to the Luftwaffe until he started his U-boat training in March 1943. Flying had taught him the value of good preparation, a highly desirable quality which he brought with him to *U1230*. Incidentally, the names Hilbig and Deecke, who landed the earlier agents in Florida, appear twice in naval records because both of them had brothers who also commanded U-boats. Jürgen Deecke commanded *U1* from October 1938 until April 1940 and Kurt Hilbig commanded *U993* and *U3526*.

A couple of days before the final approach to the American coast, U-boat Command sent a radio signal reminding Hilbig of the loss of *U1229* and urging him to be cautious. In addition to this, he was given considerable leeway to make his own final decisions on how to proceed. Everything continued to run smoothly. *U1230* was not too troubled by the enemy, took bearings on the small Porcupine Island to the northwest of Bar Harbor on Mount Desert Island and then nosed towards the shore at periscope depth. At one stage the silence was smashed by a loud clanging noise, accompanied by a clattering rasp with intermittent whistling along the boat's side. It forced the last remnants of sleep out of the crew, although it was nothing more dangerous than a collision with a whistle buoy marking the edge of the channel. At least it confirmed that *U1230* was still on the correct track.

The coming of daylight induced Hilbig to lay the boat on the seabed until darkness made progress on the surface more practical. Later, the boat was kept trimmed so low that only the conning tower showed above the water. Standing on the bridge with the first watch officer, four lookouts and the anti-aircraft crew made Hilbig feel safer than crawling through such perilous waters at periscope depth. Still, he did not take any risks and the men were armed with pistols and machine guns. There was no way the enemy was going to get into the boat until after the crew had got out and demolition charges had gone off. Yet all this precaution was unnecessary. It was a peaceful night with very little movement in the river. Both agents were rowed ashore and the inflatable dinghy was back, being stowed in its storage container less than 20min later. *U1230* simply turned round to make for the emptiness of the dark Atlantic. Everything had gone smoothly, according to plan.

The two agents vanished into bushes by the beach and made their way to the nearest road, where Colepaugh later hailed a taxi to Bangor. It was already winter and they had problems walking through the snow, made considerably worse by their long period of confinement in the U-boat and being dressed in city gear. It is rather bizarre, but the adventure could have been ended there and then by a child. A Boy Scout watched two men with suitcases enter the taxi and, thinking that this was somewhat suspicious, followed their footsteps back to the water's edge. However, when he reported this clandestine arrival to the police, no one believed him and the two spies were left in peace to continue their journey by train to Portland and then on to Boston.

Neither of them liked the idea of remaining there because it was the place where Colepaugh had lived before the war and he might be recognised. Therefore, a few days later, they continued to New York, where the bustle of the large city offered excellent anonymity. Yet, although it may sound rather far-fetched, there among the masses, Gimpel ran into a friend from his prewar years in America. Together they tried to establish a base from which to work, but constant arguments with Colepaugh had made the operation difficult and then he deserted with their gear and a good proportion of the money. Gimpel guessed where this had been hidden, though, and retrieved the suitcases from a left luggage office. This was done by showing the official the keys for the cases and being able to identify the contents. Yet, despite this run of luck, Colepaugh was arrested on 26 December 1944 to spill the beans. A thorough search for the other agent led to Gimpel's arrest just four days later. Both men were tried and sentenced to death, but their fate was commuted to life imprisonment. Gimpel returned to Germany in 1955, while Colepaugh was not released until 1960.

Chapter 5

Intrusions into Canadian Waters

LANDING LEUTNANT LANGBEIN FROM *U213*

Strangely enough it was as late as the spring of 1942, two and a half years after the beginning of the war, before the German High Command started seriously thinking about landing agents in Canada. The boat chosen for the first attempt was *U213* under ObltzS Amelung von Varendorff, a hot-headed young commander who first made his mark on history when, as second watch officer of *U47*, he was responsible for creating that famous symbol of the snorting bull on the side of the conning tower, which was later adopted by the 7th U-boat Flotilla. Prien later promoted von Varendorff to first watch officer and he held this post until shortly before *U47's* final voyage. He then went off to commanders' school and commissioned *U213* five months after Prien had disappeared.

Von Varendorff's new boat, a Type VIID, was a mechanical oddity of which only six were built. Basically it was a Type VIIC, but with an additional section aft of the conning tower accommodating vertical mineshafts. These ran straight through the pressure hull, protruding above it for over a metre to look like a box on top of the upper deck planking. The mines could be released without the boat having to surface, but there was no access to the interior of the shafts from the inside of the boat. Instead the massive free-flooding tubes featured as obstacles for anyone passing through the hull, making it necessary for men to crawl or slide around the sides. The additional length meant the boat's speed was a little inferior to a standard Type VII and responses were more sluggish.

Von Varendorff's first cruise was not successful and Dönitz was not pleased with von Varendorff's performance in the new boat, saying the application of a little more skill would have resulted in the boat not coming back empty handed from its first operational voyage.

Despite these recorded shortcomings, von Varendorff was chosen to land the first agent in Canada. Exactly how this came about is a little difficult to establish. It could well be that *U213* was selected just because the boat was ready to put to sea at the same time as the agent arrived in France. The agent was supposedly a naval artillery lieutenant named Langbein, though it is doubtful that this was his real name (the name does not feature in the *Rangliste* of naval officers) and all other identifications which have been published over the years could be aliases as well.

Langbein turned up in Lorient with a number of heavy packages and had hardly settled into the cramped surroundings when, less than three hours later, on 23 April 1942, *U213* cast off to head west into the setting sun. It was a brilliant day; such ideal flying weather that von Varendorff did not remain long on the surface. One aircraft after another forced him into the cellar, but all these chance meetings passed without incident or engagement. Despite the heavy air presence, there were no ships, so *U213* had an uneventful beginning to the voyage. Later, though, heavy head seas took their toll by ensuring that the engines used more fuel than usual.

The proximity of the Canadian coast brought back the combination of good weather and irritating aircraft frequently driving the boat into the depths. Again, *U213* was lucky that no attacks resulted. Von Varendorff thought he would need to take bearings on radio stations with the direction finder to confirm his position but this was almost a waste of time. Once he got closer to land it became apparent that navigation lights were illuminated and passing ships had lamps set according to peacetime regulations, meaning there were no navigational problems and the boat could nose into the Bay of Fundy without any difficulties.

The plan was to make landfall slightly to the northeast of Saint John in New Brunswick (not be confused with St John's of Newfoundland). The famous and unpredictable foggy weather of the Newfoundland Banks moved with *U213* to trouble the German intruders. The closer they got to the land, the worse the visibility became until finally they were hemmed in by an opaque grey curtain. It was not thick enough to obscure the most powerful lights, making navigation still relatively easy, but it added a mystical dimension to a searchlight sweeping over the water. Von Varendorff thought it was coincidence that this beam pointed towards him on numerous occasions and calmly continued with his mission by ignoring it. There were no patrol boats nor anything else to upset the undertaking.

The biggest problem came from nature, in the form of a powerful and most annoying current pushing *U213* further into the bay. The early morning visibility was cut down even further by sweeping rain, but this did not trouble the men in *U213* too much. Their first reconnaissance had been relatively successful. It was time to lay the boat on the seabed and wait for the next night.

The interior was prepared for instant destruction and no one was terribly relaxed about the prospect of spending another day in relatively shallow waters so close to the Canadian coast. Once again, it was not the enemy but the elements which annoyed the men most. The current was rotating the boat as well as scraping it along the bottom and, to make matters even worse, a noticeable rocking suggested that the weather up top was getting considerably worse. The great advantage was that there were no mechanical noises from engines or Asdic pings to interrupt the silence. The few men on duty moved about with their feet wrapped in rags to muffle footsteps. Yet, had the Canadians set up sound receivers, they might have heard von Varendorff swear. The charts he had been provided with were not good enough to establish a drop-off point and the vague orders, saying anywhere to the east of Saint John, did not help. Detailed German maps of the area were not reprinted until a couple of months after this operation, meaning that *U213* was navigating with general British charts. These were good enough for finding harbours, but failed to give any indications about the topography of the coast.

The following night, *U213* remained in the cellar until the majority of law-abiding Canadians had settled into the comfort of their beds. When the boat surfaced shortly after nightfall on 14 May 1942 to recharge batteries, fill compressed air bottles and ventilate the interior, von Varendorff found he could no longer see the coast. He knew that it was only a couple of kilometres away, so he hoped visibility was not too thick to prevent him from finding a suitable landing place. Near-vertical high cliffs observed during the first reconnaissance had

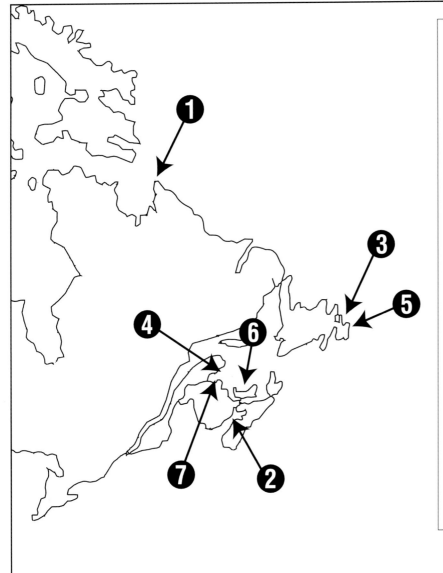

Canada

1. **Cape Chidley** - Martin's Bay 60°5'N 64°24'W
   Weather station set up by U537 - Kptlt Peter Schrewe on 22-23 October 1943

2. **Saint John**, New Brunswick
   Lieutenant Langbein landed by U213 Oblt.z.S. Amelung von Varendorff on 14 May 1942 30 miles SW of Saint John near village of St Martin

3. **Conception Bay** near Wabana
   Ships lying at anchor attacked by U518 Kptlt. Freidrich-Wilhelm Wissmann during the night 1-2 November 1942

4. **Sawyer's Point** in Chaleur Bay near New Carlisle
   Werner von Janowski landed by U518 Kptlt. Freidrich-Wilhelm Wissmann on 9 November 1942

5. **Conception Bay** near Wabana
   U513 Korvkpt Rolf Rüggeberg sunk two ships lying at anchor 5 September 1942

6. *U262 Obtlt.z.S. Heinz Franke attempted to pick up escaped prisoners of war 2 May 1943*

7. *U536 Kptlt. Rolf Schauenburg attempted to pick up escaped prisoners of war 27-28 September 1943*

not been terribly encouraging. A large inflatable dinghy was made ready on the upper deck as the boat crawled slowly towards the land, but nothing came into sight. All the lookouts could see was grey whirling mist and beyond that total blackness. There was nothing for it. Either calculation and dead reckoning had to be relied on, or the mission had to be postponed. Von Varendorff did not like either alternative, but the figures showed that the boat had to be less than 300m from the shore. It seemed pointless going back out to wait for another day when the weather could always be worse. At least the water was reasonably calm, making the final row-in relatively easy. Von Varendorff bit his lip and gave the go-ahead.

Langbein was ready. He had checked his gear, distributed it in a small number of easily carried packages and donned clean American-made underwear. He put his full naval uniform on top and then slipped into a neutral style trench coat. If he was going to be caught while landing, he wanted to be treated as a prisoner of war and not shot as a spy. However, this precaution was hardly necessary. No one interrupted his plans, making it possible to change into civilian clothing later. The second

watch officer and two seamen rowed the inflatable, but despite the lookouts' inability to see the coast, it took some 20min before the four men were finally out of sight. The slow progress was due to there being impressive vertical cliffs rising high out of the sea which looked more daunting from the insecurity of the small inflatable than from the periscope. Even if a landing spot could be found, it looked as if the steepness would prevent Langbein from climbing up. The men had only a few choices. They could either return to the submarine or continue rowing along the shore. Since the sea conditions were good, the IIWO decided upon the latter, but it still took a while before a path was spotted leading up from a tiny beach. Realising that Langbein was not going to move his gear easily on his own, the three U-boat men obliged by helping him carry it up to the top. Although they were relatively close to a major town, the place seemed totally deserted. It was now about 03.00hrs local time, meaning any potential day-trippers were still tucked up in bed.

Meanwhile, von Varendorff was experiencing problems of a different nature. The powerful current he had noted a day earlier was now threatening to wash the boat away. *U213* had

Above: The flamboyant Amelung von Varendorff who served as second and first watch officer under Kptlt Günther Prien of *U47* and was on board when the battleship HMS *Royal Oak* was sunk inside the Royal Navy's anchorage at Scapa Flow. Later he became commander of *U213* and landed the agent Leutnant Langbein in Canada. He was born on 21 December 1913 and was killed in action five months before his 30th birthday.

Above: U215, identical to *U213*, during trials in the Baltic. The front half of the boat looked similar to a Type VIIC, but there was an additional section containing a row of vertical mineshafts aft of the conning tower in this Type VIID. This lengthening of the hull also enabled the boats to carry more fuel, giving them a range of over 6,000 kilometres more than the Type VIIC. On the downside, the additional length made them less manoeuvrable and slightly slower.

to be pointed into the surge so that the electric motors could be used to hold it in position. Since he had lost sight of the dinghy, he had no idea which way the four men had gone and therefore could only remain where he was and hope that they could find the boat again. Maintaining this position was not easy and a good hour passed without the slightest sign of the landing party. Von Varendorff had established a system of light signals to help the three men back to the boat, but even flashing these into the last remnants of the night did not produce a response. It was 4hrs and 10min after departure that the first sight of the returning dinghy was reported. A deep sigh of relief indicated that a heavy weight dropped from von Varendorff's chest. The three men were quickly retrieved and *U213* headed back out to sea even before the dinghy was deflated for storage in its container. It had been a hair-raising few hours, but the men could congratulate each other on the success of a difficult mission.

Langbein was a likeable character. He had easily made friends with even the sceptics among the crew, but much of the other available information about him is so contradictory that one wonders if any of it is true. Sources seem to agree that he had worked for a number of years in Canada and only travelled back to Germany to visit his ageing parents, when the war changed whatever plans he may have had. Now, as an agent, Langbein was not expected to engage in sabotage of any kind, nor in any dangerous spying missions. Instead, the plans were for him to merge back into Canadian life and gather the sort of information on which future sabotage raids could be based. In many ways this must have seemed an ideal scheme for avoiding the rigours and dangers of war.

Having said goodbye to his companions on that cool, damp May morning, Langbein settled into an uneasy sleep until daylight allowed him to search for a good location where he could bury his case with radio transmitter and the give-away German uniform. Then, smartening himself up in his civilian clothing, he walked to the small village of St Martins. None of the shopkeepers there noticed that the banknotes he was giving them were of a design no longer in circulation and Langbein was able to slip away to Montreal and later on to Ottawa. It quickly became obvious that the masses of notes he was carrying were no longer going to buy him anything at the majority of respected shops. Therefore he had to search out more questionable establishments, where people were prepared for the hassle of exchanging the old notes at a bank. This worked relatively well, although it would seem that Langbein paid a considerable price for exchanging his high value notes for passable currency. He was lucky in other respects, too, once even being arrested in a brothel, but released again when he convinced the police that he was spending a few nights in what he thought was a boarding house.

It seems that Langbein had no intention of actually spying for Germany. He certainly had little success at establishing himself in the community. Two years later, when his money ran out and he gave himself up, no one believed his story. In the end he convinced the police by taking them to the spot where his radio and German uniform still lay buried and this may have helped to place Langbein in a detention centre, rather than a mental home, where he remained until he was repatriated to Germany after the war.

Von Varendorff and his men were not so lucky. *U213* returned to Brest in June 1942 but all aboard were killed on 31 July 1942, at the end of their next voyage, when the boat was depth charged by the sloops HMS *Erne* (Lieutenant-Commander [Lt-Cdr] E. D. Abbot), *Rochester* (Cdr

C. B. Allen) and *Sandwich* (Lt-Cdr H. Hill). This was one of those rare occasions when the blast brought considerable wreckage to the surface, including parts of bodies, making it possible to positively identify some of the victims, but there were no signs of life in any of them.

LANDING WERNER VON JANOWSKI FROM *U518*

U518 had an unusual beginning. It was a long-range boat of Type IXC, commissioned on 25 April 1942 by Fregattenkapitän (Fregkpt) Hans-Günther Brachmann, a 38-year-old from Kiel who had joined the Reichsmarine in 1922. Very little is known about him, other than that his crew did not particularly like his approach. They were virtually ready for sea, having completed their training, when a delegation of commissioned and warrant officers declared that the men were not happy about sailing with Brachmann. Personal relationships aboard U-boats were so exceptionally high on the list of priorities that men were allowed to change boats without having to give reasons. At the same time, commanders could remove anyone without formality. The delegation from *U518* therefore found a supportive ear at flotilla headquarters when they called there to list their complaints and Brachmann was removed, almost at the last moment before sailing, to be shunted into a position at the Naval High Command and Kptlt Friedrich-Wilhelm Wissmann was brought in to take the boat on its first operational voyage.

The agent *U518* was to carry, Werner von Janowski, was a happy-go-lucky type of character. In many ways he appeared to be an ideal candidate for clandestine operations. He had married in Canada before the war and lived there at his wife's expense while he trained for a variety of different jobs before returning to Europe and joining the French Foreign Legion. Later, this landed him in trouble with the police in Berlin, who considered the move to have been subversive. As a result he was unable to do very much once he returned to Germany and was even excluded from joining the armed forces. However, von Janowski eventually found a place in a special sabotage group, with which he proved himself by undertaking a number of difficult missions. By the time he made his way to Kiel for transportation to Canada, he had certainly shown the right temperament and training for the tasks ahead of him.

U518 cast off from the Tirpitz Pier in Kiel at 07.00hrs on Saturday 26 September 1942 and headed into an autumn haze hanging over a calm sea to join *U602* under Kptlt Philipp Schüler and escorts for the passage through the increasingly troublesome waters of the northwestern Baltic. Machinery and guns were tested before putting into Kristiansand in Norway for topping up fuel and water tanks. From there *U518* nosed northwards into the first signs of winter and parted company from *U602*.

A series of niggling problems then developed which included a leak with water penetrating into the boat. Although this was quite serious, it did not induce Wissmann to return to a dockyard. Running at most economical speed, he turned west to challenge the ferocity of the North Atlantic.

This was indeed a severe test. The first indications that nature was not terribly co-operative came during the afternoon of the sixth day at sea. The barometer dropped so rapidly that the men first assumed there was something the matter with it. A few hours later it became obvious that the gadget had not been broken. The calm to moderate waves gave way to a raging gale with westerly winds up to force 11. These were so severe that some men wondered whether the boat was actually making headway or whether it was being blown back to

Europe. Five days later, when the storm subsided, *U518* looked like a battered wreck, even though no contact had yet been made with enemy forces. A couple of torpedo tube doors were damaged, deck planking had been torn off, one of the periscopes was full of water, the water speed indicator did not work and there were a variety of other minor defects, all of them irritating, but none bad enough to force a turn for home.

One wonders what was going through von Janowski's mind, especially when *U518* joined a patrol line in search of a convoy. The ether kept busy, flooding in a variety of signals about action all around, but somehow Wissmann was not getting any of it. He had to wait until his 17th day at sea before a target came into sight, but this did not run within torpedo range. Instead the fast freighter made a sharp turn to vanish again over the horizon. A day later, the white inhospitable hills of Greenland appeared on the distant horizon. All attempts at repairing the attack periscope had been unsuccessful; it was fortunate that there had not been much call for it. *U518* therefore continued with the patrol, still cruising at the most economical speed. A few days later Belle Isle, guarding the northern approaches of the channel between Newfoundland and the Canadian mainland came into sight. Earlier, U-boats had reported worthwhile targets in this area, but Wissmann was not so lucky. Navigation markers were still illuminated, but there was nothing worth shooting at. On

Above: U518 under Kptlt Friedrich-Wilhelm Wissmann after landing the agent Werner von Janowski in Canada. This shows how precarious it was to work on the upper deck in rough weather. Opening the hatches in the main pressure hull would have been suicidal under such conditions. The men are struggling with a fuel pipe from the tanker *U460* to provide the necessary top-up to reach France after a successful first voyage.

19 October, he thought he had found a good target, but on closer examination it turned out to be an iceberg. At least it gave some indication of the dangers ahead.

The waning moon provided such excellent visibility at night that Wissmann decided to hang around for a couple of weeks before attempting the landing. Running ashore in such brilliant conditions was not advisable. U518 alternated between saving fuel, diving and chasing what turned out to be tiny fishing cutters. Cruising back and forth in the murk did not bring any targets and the monotony was interrupted by nothing more exciting than a rudder failure.

For some time the contraption had been showing intermittent signs of not agreeing with the boredom and early in the morning of the 32nd day at sea it protested by not responding at all. This might not have been so bad had it not been accompanied by a distinct oil trace leaving an unwelcome advert in the wake. As it so happened, these two problems were not connected and the oil trail was cured by transferring the contents into another tank. Wissmann made no further comments in his log about the rudder, so one can assume that the men got that working again. There was an emergency hand-operated wheel in the rear torpedo compartment, but relaying orders to a helmsman there, over a considerable distance through the noisy engine room, could have been tricky when at action stations.

The highlight of this period was an attack against anchored ships near Wabana in Conception Bay carried out during the night of 1/2 November 1942. Although it was midnight as U518 nosed closer to land, there were still a good number of cars racing along roads on both sides of the bay. Low clouds and a welcome sea mist provided good cover for the boat, but these helpers deserted rather suddenly. The clouds cleared, allowing the water to be illuminated by a silvery sheen. This was not the only problem. Searchlights sweeping over the sea suggested it might be better not to approach too close, but the beams stopped short and reversed, leaving U518 in peace to aim torpedoes at a number of large shadows near the shore. Exactly what happened is still difficult to ascertain. Three targets were aimed at but only two, the 7,803grt Rose Castle and 5,633grt PLM27, were sunk. Wissmann did not hang about. Turning round, he quickly made for the vastness of the open sea.

A few days later he penetrated much further into Canadian waters for the landing operation. The chosen spot was on the Quebec side of the Baie des Chaleurs near New Carlisle. The landing took place during the early hours of 9 November, while a brisk, cold southwesterly added an unwelcome dampness to the proceedings. Otherwise the weather and lighting conditions were good. A totally black night made it easy to spot illuminated houses and cars. A good number of navigation lights ensured an accurate position could be determined and everything went well, except that the men were puzzled by the liveliness of the traffic along the roads. It was well after midnight, when most roads in Germany would have calmed down for the night.

Calculations showed that it was a rising tide, so Wissmann did not expect any great problems. The only difficulty was that he could not see the beach. The entire water's edge lay in a black shadow. But that did not matter. Flooded low in the water, U518 drifted in very slowly, using the silent electric motors for the slowest speed until the keel touched the ground. Then the prepared dinghy was launched and the agent brought ashore. In silence and high tension Wissmann and his lookouts waited for the inflatable to return. It was some 700m to dry land, so the journey would take a while. Just then, at that vulnerable moment, a car stopped. As it reversed, the brilliant headlamps penetrated deep into the night and pointed towards the U-boat. Wissmann could not believe what he was seeing. The chances of something like that happening were so remote in such an isolated location. Yet, there he was, attached to Canada while a lone peasant in a car was in a position to frustrate the entire operation and perhaps even be responsible for sinking his boat. Wissmann regained his composure by the time the beam was within a few metres of the boat and he ordered the men to duck down so that their white faces could not be seen above the dull grey conning tower wall. Taking a deep breath first, Wissmann looked up. The intrusive light had gone. Virtually at the same time, the dinghy returned with the news that the agent had been landed totally dry on the beach. Everything there seemed to have been calm without interruptions. There were no problems nor any hiccups. U518 pulled astern and vanished from the scene. More than another month was to pass before the boat put in to Lorient in France. It had been a most successful trip. Not only had the agent been landed successfully, but a large number of other targets were attacked on the way back. The men had good reason to be pleased with themselves.

The biggest mistakes of the whole operation were made by the people who planned it and by Werner von Janowski himself. First, for the landing place they had chosen a seaside community which would indeed have been used to visitors in summer, but where there were hardly any new faces during the winter. Thus the agent from Germany aroused instant suspicion. This was made worse by von Janowski not being able to find a way off the beach in the dark. He was forced to remain near the water's edge, freezing in the dampness of the early winter night until daylight allowed him to escape. Burying his radio transmitter and incriminating uniform, he changed into civilian clothing before setting out to hire a room in a local hotel for a refreshing bath. Then, all manner of tiny mistakes made the landlord contact the police to arrest von Janowski before he had the chance of disappearing into the anonymity of the big towns.

The prospect of being hanged as a spy did not appeal, so he agreed to act as double agent, sending back all manner of information he was handed by the Canadian authorities. However, his minders did not get what they bargained for at first because it was quickly discovered that his radio transmitter was not powerful enough to reach Germany. Fortunately, while living in Canada before the war, von Janowski had been trained as a radio repair mechanic and thus it was plausible for him to be able to fit a booster to increase the output of his equipment. This helped a little, but the abundance of background noise in the ether still made reception difficult. Exactly what happened to him in the end is not clear, but it seems likely that he was repatriated after the war, to vanish into Europe's postwar turmoil.

DAYLIGHT RAID IN CONCEPTION BAY

U518, which dropped off Werner von Janowski, was not the first boat to make an attack on ships lying at anchor in Conception Bay. About two months earlier, U513, under Korvkpt Rolf Rüggeberg, carried out a similarly daring action during broad daylight.

Rüggeberg was born in Barcelona (Spain) in 1907 and had joined the navy in 1926, making him one of the old lags. Despite this, he was comparatively late in joining the U-boat arm. At the beginning of the war he served as a departmental head at the naval school in San Fernando, Spain and then became assistant to the naval attaché in Madrid. His submarine training lasted for only four months before he went to sea as trainee commander in *U107* under Günther Hessler (Dönitz's son-in-law). There followed one month of instruction at Deutsche Werft in Hamburg before he commissioned the brand-new *U513* on a bitterly cold January day in 1942. By contrast, it was a warm but wet August Saturday when the boat nosed out of the naval base in Kiel for its first operational tour of the war.

Once on the western side of the Atlantic, Rüggeberg astonished both the enemy and his comrades by creeping into Conception Bay and sinking the ore carriers *Lord Strathcona* (7,335grt) and *Saganaga* (5,454grt) in broad daylight. This action started just before midday on Saturday 5 September 1942 with the first of two massive explosions aboard the *Saganaga*. A couple of men, together with a good collection of deck furniture, were hurled high into the air shortly before the scene was surrounded by an astonishing cloud of smoke and flames. Less than a minute later, there was nothing left, other than bubbling water where the ship had been.

The first officer of the *Lord Strathcona*, Ross Creaser, appearing on deck at about the same time as the second torpedo struck the *Saganaga*, saw his colleagues getting one of their boats ready to pick up survivors. Quickly he ordered a message to be sent to the nearby fort, saying that there was a submarine in the bay. Then, watching the *Saganaga* disappear, he jumped into the next boat setting out to search for anyone remaining in the turbulent water. He had just left his ship when that too flew into the air to sink in less than 2minutes.

The defending forces were not so quick off the mark. By 16.00hrs there was still no sign of any retaliatory naval action, but a corvette and a submarine chaser arrived shortly afterwards for a thorough search of the bay, which lasted throughout the night. All available guns both on land and aboard ships at anchor were manned and double lookouts posted, but nothing unusual was detected. The U-boat was obviously not bold enough to come back for another attack on the remaining ships. Even so *U513* had made a big impression and this daring and impressive feat persuaded many other coastal communities to taking preventive action. Yet, despite this, more U-boats penetrated deep into Canadian waters to reap impressive harvests in the treacherous coastal shallows.

PICKING UP ESCAPED PRISONERS OF WAR

U-boats made at least two attempts to pick up escaped prisoners of war from Canadian camps. The first of these missions took place in April–May 1943 when *U262* under Heinz Franke negotiated the still heavily iced-up Cabot Strait between Newfoundland and Cape Breton Island to reach North Point on Prince Edward Island. Despite several efforts to make contact with the prospective passengers, nothing stirred and *U262* was left to turn away empty handed.

The second attempt by another boat a few months later also ended in failure, but the U-boat made a heroic effort, extracting itself from the deadly risk of being captured, only to be sunk on the European side of the Atlantic shortly before reaching base. This was *U536* under the colourful Kptlt Rolf Schauenburg, who was born in Winterthur in Switzerland in 1913. At the beginning of World War 2, he was at sea as second anti-aircraft artillery officer on the pocket battleship *Admiral Graf Spee*. Following the Battle of the River Plate, he escaped from the internment camp, made his way to Chile and from there back to Germany. After serving in destroyers for a

short time, he became watch officer and trainee commander in *U432*, shortly after her commander, Heinz-Otto Schultze, had been awarded the Knight's Cross. Although Schauenburg was on board during a period when *U432* operated off Newfoundland, he might just as well have been anywhere because there was no contact with the land.

The plan to pick up escapees had been rolling for well over a year by this time, having originally been suggested by the captured U-boat ace Otto Kretschmer through one of the letter ciphers. A variety of these were in use, with the most common one the so-called Ireland Code, given this name because it focused on the letters 'I' and 'R'. The first part of the alphabet, from A to I, represented a dot in Morse code, the second part from J to R signified a dash and the remaining letters a gap. This had not been invented as a means of organising escapes, but had been designed so that prisoners could pass sinking details and other vital intelligence to headquarters. The idea was that the message should get past censors without being noticed. The critical part of the message was the first letter of each word, making the composition of the text tedious and the results often clumsy. What was more, many users foolishly tried to conceal their code in meaningless text, which in fact made it even easier for the Allied censors to spot, so a good number of these messages were intercepted. Of course, some of the information was of use to the Allies as well, so they often allowed harmless messages to pass in order to encourage more pertinent remarks.

Below: Kptlt Heinz Franke of *U262*, who undertook a momentous voyage under ice in the Cabot Strait (Canada) to pick up escaped prisoners of war. Unfortunately, the escape failed and *U262* returned empty handed. Franke was awarded the Knight's Cross of the Iron Cross, the ribbon of which is visible around his neck, on 30 November 1943, a week before he arrived in La Pallice (France) to be handed the highly prestigious medal. The man in the leather coat on the left looks very much like KptzS Hans Rösing, Flag Officer for U-boats: West, who co-ordinated the activities in the French Atlantic bases.

Above: Loading a torpedo into the stern compartment of *U262*, a standard Type VIIC from Bremer Vulkan in Vegesack. The pole with the tripod support in the foreground was part of the loading mechanism to lower the one and a half ton torpedo slowly down the incline and would be removed before the boat put to sea.

The prisoners were being held in Camp 30 at Bowmanville near Toronto. What exactly happened will probably never be clarified, but somehow the Allies became aware of the escape plan and used the opportunity to try to capture the incoming U-boat. It would appear that two escapes took place at the same time. The major route was a 300-metre-long tunnel, which the Canadian guards later described as a masterpiece of engineering. The other involved a single U-boat commander, Wolfgang Heyda, scaling a high tension electricity cable with improvised climbing irons and using a makeshift bosun's chair to pull himself over the camp's perimeter fence. The tunnellers, including Otto Kretschmer, Horst Elfe and Hans Ey, were captured exceedingly quickly, but the authorities were unaware of Heyda's lone effort until he was missed at roll-call. Consequently he succeeded in making his way within a kilometre or so of the pick-up point. At that stage, the Allies shot themselves in the foot by arresting him. Had they let him go, he might have sent the correct code to draw the U-boat inshore. Instead, the Allies sent a signal in plain language telling U536 to come closer, which made Schauenburg suspicious, turn and run for the open sea.

The pick-up point, Pointe de Maisonette in New Brunswick, was located on the shallow northfacing shore of Chaleur Bay, opposite New Carlisle where Werner von Janowski had been landed by U518. At this point, a good 50km inland from the Gulf of St Lawrence, the bay was some 25km wide. These dimensions make it a massive expanse of water when one looks at it from the cliffs or tries sailing it in a dinghy, but to a U-boat crew it could only seem incredibly confined once a number of warships threatened to sweep it in a well-rehearsed search pattern.

Unlike Heinz Franke in U262, Rolf Schauenburg had been briefed before leaving base, although none of his men knew what was happening until a few minutes before the pick-up. The reason for this exceptional security was the high risk of the boat being sunk and the men falling into Allied hands. In such an event, there were a number of other boats at sea with sealed envelopes containing details of the operation, to be drawn into the intrigue at the last minute, as U262 had been.

Approaching the pick-up point was not easy. U536 spotted an unusually high number of aircraft and fast warships. On top of this, at about the time they entered the wide bay, lookouts reported several destroyers in the far distance. No wonder the Canadian navy was intent on capturing the U-boat. There was no way they intended to allow it back out to sea. The idea was to catch it in shallow water, at that vulnerable moment when it was almost stranded on the beach. Although U536 did get within a couple of hundred metres of the shore, Schauenburg was not the type to trust his luck. The small stretches of coast

Above: The bows of U262. There was very little space to walk around and the gun had to be swung sideways to make room. This operation was quite tricky when performing it on a good day in port. Imagine the problems when having to reload torpedoes in rough, cold weather at sea.

he had seen reflected a busy almost peacetime atmosphere, with navigation lights visible, illuminated windows in houses, and cars with their headlamps on. Only the destination was bathed in a deep black calmness, which did not look right. Then, instead of the recognition signal, came the words 'Komm Komm' (meaning 'come come'). At the same time a brilliant display of Northern Lights, shooting over the bay, reflected across the mirror-smooth surface of the water. Schauenburg was cautious and immediately dived out of the way. There was not much room below the keel, but Morse messages without the recognised code were too much in such bright illumination. Seconds later depth charges started booming through the water — a good long way away, but unnerving all the same. U536 had not been spotted and there were no other U-boats in the area, so why drop depth charges? At the same time noises of surface ships started coming closer. Someone, somewhere was panicking, suggesting to Schauenburg that it was time to withdraw.

Below: U262 with men loading ammunition for the 88mm quick firing deck gun. The shells were protected by tubes with firmly sealed ends and were stored in a locker underneath the radio room. Once at sea it would have been too dangerous to open the torpedo hatch in the main deck because the top of the pressure hull would have been very close to the surface of the water and there was always the danger of water washing down into the boat. Therefore ammunition was brought up through the conning tower, down again at the back and then carried around the side to the front. The thin stalk-shaped object in the front to the right of the jumping wire is the head of an underwater sound detection system and a couple of bollards are visible on the left.

Above: U262 showing a torpedo being lowered into the stern compartment.

The signal 'Kebitz verpfiffen', meaning 'Operation Lapwing blown', was sent back to headquarters after Schauenburg had extracted his boat from a most precarious predicament. Had he done the expected thing, that is turn round and head back out of the bay, he would almost certainly have been caught in the trap, but Schauenburg had escaped twice before while on the run from internment in South America and he knew that he must do the one thing which was not expected of him. In this case it was to creep closer to the shore, remain silent and use the shallows to hide his boat. The trick worked, despite the submarine pulling up a number of fixed fishing nets. The hunters continued searching the deep water, plastering *U536's* escape route with depth charges, but they were unlucky. *U536* made it out into the open Atlantic to hunt in deeper waters off Canada for another two weeks before heading east to join the Schill 2 patrol line.

However, on the night of 19/20 November, more than a month after the ill-fated pick-up attempt, *U536* fell foul of convoy escorts. Depth charges from HMS *Nene* (Cdr J. D. Birch), HMCS *Snowberry* (Lt J. Dunn) and HMCS *Calgary* (Lt-Cdr H. Hill) brought the boat to the surface and destruction, but Schauenburg and 16 men survived to tell the story of how they beat the Canadians in the shallows of their own coast.

THE GERMAN BASE IN CANADA

Germany's one and only base on the American continent remained hidden until the early 1980s, but then its discovery unravelled itself in an even stranger manner than the original instalment. The story started when KptzS aD (ausser Dienst) Otto Köhler, the first commander of *U377*, was beginning to enjoy his retirement in Freiburg, on the edge of the Black Forest. There he met up with an old wartime associate, Dr Kurt Sommermeyer, whom he had ferried to Spitzbergen in 1942. My father participated in those expeditions as the boat's chief diesel engineer. He left the boat after the 12th operational cruise, but was recalled because the other chief engineer was taken ill and *U377* could not go out with two new hands in the

Above: This shows *U262* with the improved anti-aircraft armament. The upper gun platform has been enlarged, but it appears that only one twin 20mm has been fitted, which is unusual because most boats had two of these somewhat ineffective weapons. A bottle containing hydrogen has been strapped to the outside of the conning tower between the men on the *Wintergarten* and the slightly extended rod aerial. This was used for filling the balloons for the radar decoy. This device trailed a length of string with a floating weight at the end and several strips of metal foil along its length. These reflected radar impulses to produce a similar echo to that of a surfaced submarine. The head of the extended circular radar warning aerial, to the left of the rod aerial, can hardly be made out because it blends with the background.

The shield at the front of the conning tower, showing a winged dagger, was the emblem of the Luftwaffe's 2nd Hunter-Group East, who were trained near La Pallice where *U262* was stationed. One of the officers presented *U262* with one of their emblems as a sign of friendship, which the U-boat then carried into battle. The black aircraft with the date 8.8.43 indicate that the boat succeeded in shooting down two enemy aircraft. The five rings are the emblem of Crew 36, the year of the Olympic Games in Germany and the time when Kptlt Heinz Franke joined the navy.

The boat must have been through a pretty hard time because the jumping wire running down from the top of the conning tower to the bows is missing. Franke, with the white cap, is holding a megaphone in his left hand.

engine room. Therefore, my father was on board for the last fateful voyage in January 1944, three months before I was born, when *U377* disappeared. Köhler was fortunate in having been promoted in the meantime to head the navy's new acoustic torpedo school and thus survived the war.

That meeting in Freiburg spurred Köhler to suggest that Dr Sommermeyer might have some photographs of my father, but unfortunately this interesting link was quickly broken by the doctor's untimely death. However, his son, Klaus, helped by sending a box of photographs, suggesting that I might find some of my father among them. These pictures included one rather interesting shot of what looked like a radio transmitter with an aerial from the Canadian Weather Service. The coal mining settlements on Spitzbergen, where my father had been with *U377*, had been evacuated by Allied forces earlier in the war and a group of Canadians had stayed behind to keep the radio station operational in order to conceal the event from the Germans; hence the mast and its inscription seemed to fit very well into that story.

Later, however, I showed the picture to the Austrian-born engineer, Franz Selinger, whose study of German Arctic weather stations had made him the undisputed expert in this subject. He agreed that the strange structure was indeed an automatic weather station, but did not recognise the location as being Spitzbergen. Further research suggested that the station was somewhere in northern Canada, but the authorities there informed Selinger that he was mistaken. They told him that there had never been a German base in Canada. A postal strike added considerable delays to the correspondence and the Canadian reply arrived shortly after Selinger had discovered the identity of the U-boat which had installed the equipment and thus found the position from the logbook. This gave him the splendid satisfaction of shattering the arrogance encapsulated in the official reply. Later it led to an invitation to visit the site with the aim of possibly recovering some artefacts for a museum display.

Now, at this stage, it may be of interest to slip back to the autumn of 1943, when the German Meteorological Service built a number of automatic weather stations for installation in the Arctic by U-boats. This mode of transport added to the construction difficulties because the entire structure had to dismantle for fitting into containers which could pass through small circular hatches. The prototypes, tried out in the harshness of the Erz Mountains, worked well, suggesting that they should go into production. Two of them were built for Canada, but one of them never arrived. *U867* under KptzS Arved von Mühlendahl was first badly damaged by a Mosquito from 248 Squadron RAF, piloted by H. A. Corbin. The British radio monitors then intercepted a distress call asking for tug assistance. Unable to dive, the U-boat crew waited patiently and even put up a considerable burst of anti-aircraft fire when a Liberator from 224 Squadron RAF was sent to attack. Flight Lieutenant H. J. Rayner's depth charges overshot by such a distance that he did not think they could have seriously damaged the boat, but on circling he was surprised to see the crew abandoning ship and then he noticed the target settling lower in the water until it disappeared on an even keel, suggesting it had been scuttled. Sadly, none of the survivors in the inflatables reached land alive. *U867* was sunk on 18 September 1943.

The other Canadian weather station was carried by *U537* under Kptlt Peter Schrewe (who should not be confused with Georg Schewe of *U60* and *U105*). Dr Sommermeyer and his assistant, Walter Hildebrandt, arrived in Kiel with their equipment towards the middle of September 1943 and the boat then called at Bergen in Norway before crossing over to Labrador. The timing was critical. The plan was to install the device shortly before the sea froze over for the winter and thus prevent the Canadians from reaching the spot for months if they discovered its location with direction finders. Unknown to the Germans, even this was highly unlikely because the Canadian authorities only took bearings on transmitters out at sea and hardly searched for signals from the land-based locations.

Once again, as had been the case with other landings, the operation was not given highest priority and *U537* spent some time in Icelandic waters for the radio operators to send a chain of prearranged signals, imitating the presence of a heavy surface squadron. This went relatively well, but the men in *U537* did not have an easy time. A leak in the engine room, not serious enough for turning round, added to their problems and a patch of the most appalling weather made a good number seriously seasick. The conditions were so bad that they ripped the 20mm quadruple anti-aircraft gun from the lower *Wintergarten* behind the conning tower. In addition to this, both periscopes were flooded, one diesel engine developed a fault, and there were numerous other minor problems. Schrewe contemplated turning round, but his engineering officer assured him that the faults could be repaired on the western side of the Atlantic, when the boat was moored in calm coastal waters.

The weather remained abominable, making the two meteorologists wish they had volunteered for some less physically demanding and nerve-racking undertaking. Yet, despite this seemingly endless chain of natural disasters, almost worse than the ferocity of depth charge attacks, neither Schrewe nor his men gave up. Finding the destination was not at all easy because blinding snowstorms for the best part of a week had not only whipped up the water into mountainous seas, but also obscured the natural navigation aids, making it impossible to see sun or stars. The Obersteuermann had to rely on dead reckoning. However, this was not as bad as it might seem — after all finding Canada was not particularly difficult and it did not matter exactly where they landed, as long as it was in a remote spot, and such places are rather abundant along that long stretch of desolate Arctic coast.

Shortly after midday on 22 October 1943, lookouts sighted Cape Chidley at the entrance to the Hudson Strait and soon afterwards Schrewe started taking soundings to make sure that they would not bump into anything unexpected. Schrewe was determined not to make the mistakes of the past. Progress was fast and it did not take long before the anchor was dropped in Attinaukjuke Bay, a native name which has been anglicised as Martin Bay. Its position is about 60°5'N 64°24'W. Within an hour, a reconnaissance party was sent ashore together with a bag of specially prepared Canadian litter such as cigarette packets and emergency ration tins captured from crashed aircraft. This little extra was thought to be a good idea; if the station happened to be found it might not be reported to anyone who knew better if it looked as if it was a Canadian one.

The temperature was only two degrees below freezing with little wind, suggesting it was best to make use of the unexpectedly good conditions. Therefore, without hesitation, the men set to work. Less than three hours after arriving they started ferrying the heavy containers ashore with the aid of a large inflatable. At the same time, the technical division repaired the damage inside the U-boat. Although there was more than enough for everybody to do, Schrewe thought it wise to take the additional precaution of posting lookouts on high ground, just in case the location was not as isolated as he had imagined.

Everything went well, the weather station with its radio mast and batteries was taken ashore, set up and soon afterwards transmitted its first signal. The men were delighted. Some 28 hours after arriving, *U537* weighed anchor and headed back out to sea. The radio room kept monitoring the station, but the men were surprised to hear the signals being jammed. They were even more astonished when they learned that this interference came from the German rather than the Allied side. Yet, there was nothing they could do about it other than complain, but even that had to wait until they were further away. It would be some time before *U537* felt safe enough to send the success signal back to base.

The acknowledgement for the success signal came with the welcome permission for Schrewe to have a totally free hand to operate anywhere in Canadian waters, but he was warned not to stray into a minefield near St John's recently laid by *U220* under Kptlt Bruno Barber. *U537* did not stumble upon any

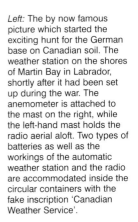

Left: The by now famous picture which started the exciting hunt for the German base on Canadian soil. The weather station on the shores of Martin Bay in Labrador, shortly after it had been set up during the war. The anemometer is attached to the mast on the right, while the left-hand mast holds the radio aerial aloft. Two types of batteries as well as the workings of the automatic weather station and the radio are accommodated inside the circular containers with the fake inscription 'Canadian Weather Service'.

Above: The heavy batteries also acted as anchors for the two masts, to prevent them from being blown over by the wind.

Right: A close-up of the mast with wind and temperature sensors on the top.

Above: U537 under Kptlt Peter Schrewe which carried the automatic weather station to Canada and helped the two meteorologists to set it up.

Above: U537 anchored in Martin Bay, northern Canada.

Above: U537 shortly after arriving in Martin Bay, northern Canada. The voyage across the Atlantic had been so rough that the large quadruple 20mm anti-aircraft gun on the lower platform was ripped from its foundation to vanish into the depths.

Above: Keeping lookout ashore was a sought-after job and even the commander and engineering officer took turns to sit by the water's edge with heavy machine guns at the ready. There were two more men further up on the high cliffs to make certain nothing would creep up on the anchored U-boat.

Above: The engineering officer LtzS Günter Graeser taking a breather to feel Canadian soil under his feet. He only went ashore for a brief period because there was plenty for him to do on board, repairing damage sustained during the earlier heavy storm.

targets, though, and returned without sinking anything. However, Schrewe did succeed in bringing the two meteorologists safely to Lorient, where he arrived on 8 December 1943. Three months later, *U537* left again for the Indian Ocean, arrived in Batavia in August 1944 and was then sunk with all hands in the Java Sea during the following November while on the way back to Europe.

It seems that *U537's* efforts were worth while because the station did transmit the required data, and this success prompted an attempt to plant another such station by *U867* in the same area a year later. Following the loss of this boat, no further efforts were made to establish a base in Canada, since by then the war was almost over.

The weather station, code named 'Kurt', was not discovered until 1981, when Franz Selinger gave the news of its existence to the Canadian authorities. Following this, he was invited to join a small exploration group made up of Dr W. A. B. Douglas (Director of History at the National Defence Headquarters), Captain Jim Clarke (Director of Fleet Systems of the Canadian Coast Guard) and Donna C. Andrew (Public Relations Officer) to investigate the site at close quarters. Canadian Air Force reconnaissance flights had confirmed that it definitely was still there, but the discovery was considered important enough for a closer on-the-spot examination.

The icebreaker *Louis S. St Laurent* under Capt M. S. Tanner quickly established that Schrewe had either been especially lucky, brave or foolhardy to approach so close. The icebreaker did not take the risk of repeating his feat, remained moored a long way off the hazardous pack-ice and used its helicopter to bring the explorers to the weather station. Sadly, much of it had been destroyed, with bits and pieces scattered over a large area. At first it was thought that nomadic Eskimos had vandalised the canisters, but later it was thought that they would not have had the tools for dismantling everything so neatly. Some parts of the weather station were brought back by the icebreaker for making into a museum display. A report published in Canada later produced a response from a group of geomorphologists who had discovered the site earlier, but left it intact, thinking it was part of the official establishment, but this verified that the break-up of the equipment had taken place relatively shortly before the arrival of the recovery team, although how this happened is not known.

Below: Men on *U537* shooting the sun to ascertain an accurate position. The third watch officer, LtsZ Freudenberg is looking through the binoculars.

Above: U537's first watch officer, Bruno Dieck, shooting the sun with a sextant.

Above: Lookout aboard U537.

Above: Second watch officer, Harold Eberhard, who was killed on 9 November 1944, sporting U537's emblem on his cap showing an anchor with two crossed daggers. This type of cap, known as *Schiffchen* or small ship type, was favoured because it folded flat and thus occupied very little space in the cramped interior of the boat.

Right: Harold Eberhard wearing U537's Ice Medal. Ideally the men would have loved to have called it the Canadian Labrador Medal, but security prevented them from disclosing any connection with the American mainland.

Chapter 6
Along the Fringes of the Sahara

LANDING JEAN LALLART FROM *U66*

The prospects of taking command of *U66* filled Kptlt Friedrich Markworth with considerable trepidation. Life would have been much easier had he been given the option of going back to Germany to commission a brand-new boat. Instead he was told to remain in France and take over on 22 June 1942 from Kptlt Richard Zapp, a knight of the Iron Cross. Zapp had already taken *U66* into the North Atlantic, to the Freetown area of Africa, to the United States and twice to the Caribbean, an incredible series of accomplishments for any new commander to live up to. Of course, there were also distinct advantages with a run-in boat, but the general prospects were quite intimidating. Inexperienced newcomers were likely to face a considerable ego collapse. Markworth knew that better men than himself had been left in serious doubt as to who actually was in charge. He knew that he could look forward to those unsettling moments when seamen with no rank might censure his actions. There was, for example, an incident when one of the crew ordered *U178* to dive as a result of watching his commander eye up an approaching aircraft. As soon as the hive of activity calmed down in the depths, Hans Ibbeken yelled at the offender, 'Who the hell do you think is commanding this boat?' The man, hardly ruffled by his superior, replied calmly, 'No one is challenging your position, but if you want to remain alive, then you need to think and react just a little bit faster.'

Despite a wealth of potential problems, Markworth found a supportive atmosphere in *U66*, easing him smoothly through his baptism of fire. This was indeed not easy. Not only did he have to contend with an exceptionally long voyage to the Caribbean, to lay mines at Castries on Saint Lucia, but on the way back he was faced with a most unusual problem. This came about as a result of a refuelling from *U462* under ObltzS Bruno Vowe. It was one of those issues one could laugh about afterwards over a glass of wine, but at the time it was like a bombshell, threatening to leave *U66* floundering in the dangerous Bay of Biscay without power.

This potential disaster came about because oil floats on water. The bottoms of fuel tanks were open to the sea so that water could replace the oil as it was used up. That way, there was no danger of explosive gases forming or bubbles interfering with diving procedures. On this particular occasion, no one realised that most of the oil on *U462* had already been consumed and for much of the time seawater was being pumped from one submarine to another. The period of blissful ignorance would even have been prolonged had the engineer officer not insisted on a thorough check before heading back into more dangerous waters, but by then the damage was done. *U66* was already too far away from the supply boat.

Below: Commissioning *U66* on 2 January 1941 at Deschimag AG Weser in Bremen. Although the Type IX boats are often referred to as being 'large', they were still tiny when compared to even small ocean-going merchantmen. This picture clearly shows how *U66* is dwarfed by the ship behind it.

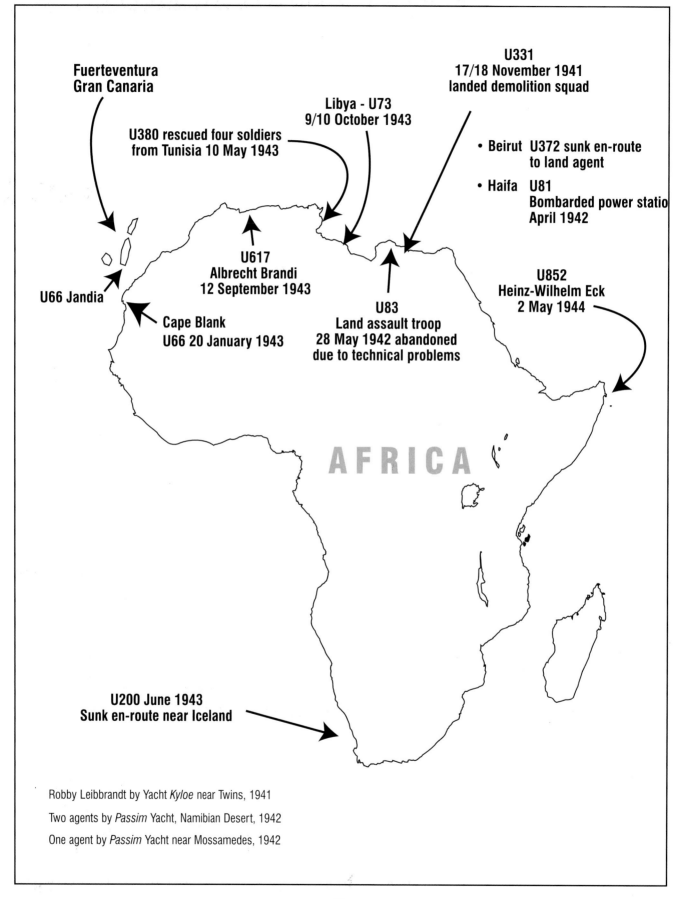

Fuerteventura
Gran Canaria

U331
17/18 November 1941
landed demolition squad

U380 rescued four soldiers
from Tunisia 10 May 1943

Libya - U73
9/10 October 1943

• Beirut U372 sunk en-route
to land agent

• Haifa U81
Bombarded power statio
April 1942

U66 Jandia

U617
Albrecht Brandi
12 September 1943

Cape Blank
U66 20 January 1943

U83
Land assault troop
28 May 1942 abandoned
due to technical problems

U852
Heinz-Wilhelm Eck
2 May 1944

AFRICA

U200 June 1943
Sunk en-route near Iceland

Robby Leibbrandt by Yacht *Kyloe* near Twins, 1941

Two agents by *Passim* Yacht, Namibian Desert, 1942

One agent by *Passim* Yacht near Mossamedes, 1942

No one knew for sure exactly how far the boat could still manage, but it looked highly possible that progress would come to an abrupt halt in the danger zone of the Bay of Biscay, which was under tight surveillance by aircraft from Coastal Command. There was no way that Markworth could risk proceeding with a return voyage which would almost certainly end with the boat's destruction. On the other hand, there was also no point in staying in the relative safety of what remained of the Mid-Atlantic Air Gap because there were no other boats in the vicinity. Drastic action had to be taken. U-boat Command went into emergency mode and made arrangements for U66 to be secretly refuelled in neutral Spain.

Such a landfall in a foreign harbour was a major undertaking in itself, especially when one remembers that Markworth had little practice at mooring his 1,000 tons of steel in a strange place and in total darkness reached by sailing through confined shallow waters with ample opportunity to bump into all manner of obstacles. Having reached the destination, U66 waited on the seabed outside El Ferrol for night to fall. Only then did U66 surface and creep cautiously through the darkness towards a set of distinctive lights, though distinguishing the prearranged signals from the supply ship, Max Albrecht, among this background clutter was not easy.

Yet it worked and Markworth brought his boat back to France. His second voyage almost ended in disaster as well when a practice deep-dive shortly after leaving France brought the Bay of Biscay flooding in. It was only the quick thinking of the engineering officer which brought the boat back to the surface for the pumps to expel the offending sea. There was no choice. Markworth could only turn the boat round and head home as fast as possible, hoping he could reach Lorient before the Royal Air Force prevented further progress. There was no way he could dive without inviting more seawater into the interior, and this was likely to enter considerably faster than the ballast pumps could force it out again.

There was nothing for it other than to convert the upper deck into a storage area for ammunition and hope that a brilliant display would fend off any potential attackers. U66 was lucky that new anti-aircraft guns had been fitted shortly before this voyage; therefore the men could put up a reasonable response. The Royal Air Force had not yet fully appreciated the new punch carried by the U-boats and many pilots still came too close, thinking they were facing the ineffective fire of earlier days. So there was a chance. U66 was in fact caught at night by a Leigh Light aircraft, but succeeded in outmanoeuvring its depth charges.

The damage which had caused the leak took the best part of two months to repair. This gave the crew an opportunity of attending an anti-aircraft gun course and going home for Christmas, so it was early in January 1943 before U66 set out once more, this time with a secret agent on board for one of those titillating special operations. The basic plan was quite simple, except that things always turned out differently from the way they had been conceived on paper. All Markworth had to do was to drop off the one man, Jean Lallart, near Cape Blanc in Mauritania. This was under control of the Free French authorities and the neutral territory of Spanish Morocco was not too far away as a convenient bolt hole if things did not go too well with the French.

Markworth and his men knew little of Africa but he had read that an incredibly powerful surf discouraged the people of the Western Sahara from supplementing their living with fishing. These waves were so big and powerful that it was often impossible for small boats to get through. The advantage was that there were hardly any harbours; therefore U66 was unlikely to be troubled by coastal traffic.

The initial reconnaissance did not produce any evidence of shipping nor surf. An intense heat haze over the beaches did not show up anything other than desolation decorated with rocks and wind-blown sand dunes. Seeing this for the first time through the periscope under the midday sun, Markworth decided to drift with the current of the Atlantic swell until a suitably secluded landing place could be found. A sandy bay, hidden from general view by a few cliffs and without noticeable rocks, would be ideal. Such a combination was not long in coming. Less than three hours later he spotted the ideal location. Grasping the opportunity, he allowed the boat to rest on the seabed until it was dark enough to attempt the landing. The agent prepared himself after his long spell of confinement and two good swimmers, Bootsmaat Wagner and Matrosenobergefreiter Daschkey, were briefed to row him ashore.

This part of the operation had not been rehearsed and a good number of the crew threw in their advice. The plan was to take an inflatable dinghy with an anchor and a long length of rope, thin enough so that it could be thrown over a considerable distance. It was quite likely that the men were going in for an enforced swim and Markworth thought it would be a good idea for them to have some means of fishing themselves out again if the boat capsized.

It was 20.00hrs on 20 January 1943 when U66 was eased off the bottom to move slowly towards the coast. The first snag was not long in coming. Having reached a shallow depth of 20m under the keel, the men found they were still some two kilometres from the beach, but conditions were good and neither Wagner nor Daschkey seemed perturbed by the distance. Markworth told Wagner not to go through the surf if this proved too difficult. Instead he was to let the agent swim ashore. After all, it was warm and his clothing would dry pretty quickly once the intense tropical heat got to work during the following day.

There was the remote possibility that the dinghy might get ashore, but not back again. Therefore Markworth took the precaution of devising a contingency plan. He told the men to walk in the direction of Cape Blanc and then swim back to the boat if the surf pinned the dinghy to the beach. All this appeared to be somewhat superfluous because there was no sight nor sound of any noteworthy waves. What Markworth failed to do was to establish a signalling system, leaving the men in the dinghy incapable of communicating with the U-boat.

Despite this, everything went smoothly. Exceptionally bright moonlight made it possible for lookouts on the conning tower to watch the dinghy go ashore. It was only after the men had reached land, when they pulled the inflatable into the shadow of some rocks, that the lookouts lost sight of them. But this was understandable. Even if the place was deserted, there was no point standing around advertising their presence, though Markworth could not understand why Wagner and Daschkey did not just abandon the agent and row back. Perhaps their long period of inactivity in the submarine had sapped their strength and they needed a few minutes to recover from the strenuous exercise? Minutes of tension dragged by exceptionally slowly, but the dinghy did not reappear.

Using powerful night-glasses, lookouts saw the agent make off up the dunes and disappear from sight. Although there was no other noticeable movement, Markworth was not unduly perturbed. Some 10min later, when the agent was seen to be returning, there was a stunning change in circumstances. The gentle lapping of calm waves suddenly erupted into the most

Left: U66 probably photographed while leaving for the last voyage under Richard Zapp. The two poles sticking up from the conning tower on the right are the commander's flagpole (right) and the partly extended rod aerial (left).

Right: 23 June 1942, the day when *U66* left for her first voyage to the Caribbean under Kptlt Friedrich Markworth, who can be seen wearing the white cap. Next to him is ObltzS Siebold and on the bottom right Obersteuermann Fröhlich.

Above: One of *U66's* inflatable dinghies photographed in mid-Atlantic early in September 1942, while refuelling from the supply boat *U462* under Kptlt Bruno Vowe. The dinghy used to land the agent on the fringes of the Sahara was similar to this one

Left: U66 safely back in port after Markworth's baptism of fire. The trip to the Caribbean had not been easy, but was quite successful, although one man died at sea from illness before he could be brought to hospital for treatment. In the original photograph it is possible to make out that the single medal on Markworth's left breast is the Iron Cross First Class. Two bollards can be seen in the background, near the bows. Between them and the crew is the head of the electric winch, which was used to tighten the mooring lines.

Right: Oberfunkmaat (Radio Petty Officer) Hannes Hildebrand of *U66*. Note that the rim of the hatch in which he is standing is not horizontal. Therefore this is one of the torpedo loading hatches. The object on the extreme right is of special interest. It appears to be a large mirror reflecting the conning tower of a boat, but it is difficult to explain what *U66* would have been doing with such a reflector. Or could it be a large photograph?

Left: It seems likely that this is the same hatch as in the previous photograph, the entrance to the stern torpedo room, but there is no submarine moored to the left. So the theory of the large mirror, mentioned in the caption for the previous picture, falls flat.

Above: The central control room of *U66*. The man in the middle is standing at the bottom of the ladder leading up into the conning tower, and the end of a speaking tube can be made out on the top left. The two men sitting on the left are operating the hydroplane controls.

Above: The type of view men from *U66* would have seen while carrying out their first reconnaissance of the African coast. Much of the scenery there is dominated by sand blown over rocks to produce an ever-changing landscape, making it exceedingly difficult to recognise certain spots over a period of time unless one knows them well.

Right: Two men carrying out running repairs on *U66's* upper deck under conditions which would make it exceedingly difficult, or even impossible, to launch a dinghy.

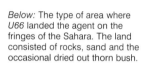

Below: The type of area where *U66* landed the agent on the fringes of the Sahara. The land consisted of rocks, sand and the occasional dried out thorn bush.

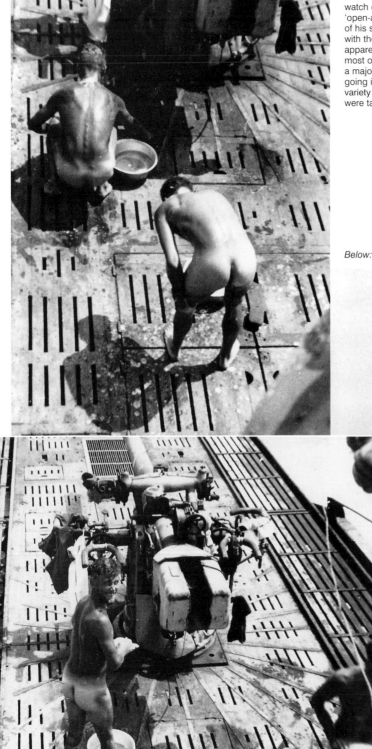

Left: Friedrich Markworth, while first watch officer of *U103*, using the 'open-air bathroom'. The dark colour of his skin contrasts considerably with the other man whose duties apparently kept him down below for most of the time. Being sunburnt was a major problem for crews of boats going into southern waters and a variety of different creams and oils were taken along to combat it.

Below: Friedrich Markworth keeping lookout while serving aboard *U103*.

Above: Friedrich Markworth washing with seawater by the side of the 105mm quick firing gun while serving as first watch officer of *U103*. Although having a higher number, *U103* was a Type IXB, while *U66*, Markworth's first command, was a Type IXC. However, the heavy guns and the appearance of the decks were similar.

chaotic froth. It was impossible to bring the small dinghy back through the fierce barrier, now erupting like a series of fountains. Such conditions were probably caused by a change in the tide, but the men in *U66* had not taken this possibility into account.

At 04.00hrs, almost six hours after the launch, when there was still no sign of activity ashore Markworth ordered a message to be flashed by signal lamp. He tried the instruction, 'Walk along the beach,' hoping to establish exactly where the men had got to. There was no response. Three hours later, when there was still no sight of dinghy or men, the first signs of daylight made him pull the boat back into deeper water. The footsteps and the trail, where the boat had been dragged, remained as the only indication of the nocturnal intrusion.

Resting at periscope depth, lookouts in *U66* kept the landing beach in sight, but it remained just as deserted as it had been at first light. At 11.00hrs Markworth decided that the location was isolated enough to risk surfacing in daylight, with a view to crawling along the coast towards a headland where the men might be waiting. Nothing was seen. *U66* returned to the landing beach at first light the following day and then, once again, slowly moved along the coast, searching. A number of fishing boats with Canary Islands markings invaded the tranquillity of the peaceful desolation but there was nothing else; no men, no signs of any activity. The only real threat came an hour or so before darkness when an aircraft flew overhead, but it looked as if it was using the coast as a means of navigating and showed no interest in the U-boat.

Having waited so long without results, Markworth could only think that his men might have been surprised by French troops and captured. Or was there something preventing them from getting back through the surf? Perhaps they walked inland with the agent? Whatever, *U66* could not hang around for ever and eventually left with deep disappointment.

In fact Wagner and Daschkey had indeed been captured. Postwar reports have suggested that this happened because their dinghy had capsized but the strange point is that none of the lookouts saw this. Apparently it was a bright night and the boat's progress was clearly visible. Perhaps the men had become weary of war and decided to throw in the towel. Whatever, they were arrested by French authorities, probably as a result of the agent giving himself up at the nearest military outpost. Ten days after the landing, on 30 January 1943, Markworth received a signal from Naval Intelligence telling him that all three men had been made prisoners of war.

There is rather an interesting postscript to this story, although that has nothing to do with this particular incident. Having landed the agent and lost two of his crew, Markworth joined the Rochen Pack and was due to have been refuelled from *U461* (Kptlt Wolf-Harro Stiebler) near the Azores when another convoy was sighted. Consequently the refuelling was postponed and *U66* was directed towards the Canary Islands. Shortly before first light on 3 February lookouts sighted the last flashes of the night from the lighthouse at Jandia. Almost instantly, the dark and jagged outline of the Fuerteventuran mountains could be made out against the slightly lighter sky. Moving westwards, the men ascertained their exact position more definitely by also taking a bearing on the light at Isleta, the northern tip of Gran Canaria.

Minutes later, with dawn breaking over its stern, *U66* came within sight of the Villa Winter near Cofete, since reputed to have been a secret U-boat base. Action against an abundance of convoys continued unabated all around but a shortage of provisions finally caused *U66* to head back to France. Yet, there she was, in need of supplies, and within minutes of what has been described as a major underground refuelling centre. So why not use it? Or is this one more piece of evidence that such a facility did not exist? The existence or otherwise of this base will be discussed more fully in Chapter 8.

MEDITERRANEAN LANDINGS

The north African coast of the Mediterranean provided totally different conditions to the vast emptiness of the Atlantic shores. Korvkpt Wilhelm Dommes, who is most famous for having set up U-boat bases in the Far East and who gained his Knight's Cross under the oppressive restrictions of the Mediterranean, said that the only way to survive there was for the commander to have the entire chart in his head. The uncomfortable heat, crystal clear shallow water, often with a mirror-smooth surface, and usually excellent visibility, combined with the close proximity of land made the Mediterranean an exceptionally difficult battleground for submarines. Some of the action there forced U-boats into coastal waters, where they endured conditions none of them had been trained for. *U431*, for example, touched Africa more than most boats, providing too many occasions when Dommes could see tree-fringed beaches through his periscope.

Kptlt Friedrich Guggenberger, who sunk the British aircraft carrier *Ark Royal*, went one better by actually aiming his guns at land targets. Although it may sound absurd, a power station in Palestine offered a good opportunity. Unlike their north European counterparts, here the machinery was built out in the open without the protection of a large building. Therefore *U81* could inflict considerably more damage than just irritating the night watchmen. Shells from the 88mm deck gun brought the plant to a standstill, depriving the occupying British troops of essential power.

It is also noteworthy that the Mediterranean has thrown up a large concentration of mystery attacks. U-boat log books contain a good number of incredibly vivid accounts of sinkings, describing how men observed vast fireballs, watched parts of ships fly through the air and saw hulks disappear below the waves. Yet, a large proportion of these have never been accounted for in Allied records and have not yet been identified. The same can be said for the landings on Mediterranean shores. It appears that there were a good number, but the majority seem either to have gone unrecorded or the records have been scrapped.

One special mission which definitely took place fell to *U73* under Kptlt Horst Deckert, who ferried a man, disguised as a shipyard worker, from La Spezia to Algeria in October 1943. Everything seems to have been well prepared and the operation went so smoothly that some men inside the boat might hardly have noticed, had it not been got ready for quick destruction. The reason for this was that there was a good chance of being disabled in shallow waters and the U-boat Command wanted to prevent too much of value falling into enemy hands. Therefore, special scuttling charges, with time delay fuses, were attached to the torpedoes, not only to sink the boat but also to blow it and all its secrets to pieces.

The agent, dressed in a British major's uniform, rowed ashore on his own and flashed the green light of his torch several times to indicate that everything had gone well. Deckert did not hang around. Instantly the diesels sprang to life and *U73* made off fast, never to hear anything about the incident again. Since the men had been sworn to special secrecy, the subject was not discussed either. So as far as they were concerned the incident had never taken place and they concentrated on finding targets in slightly deeper waters.

U73 was a lucky boat. It survived 17 operational cruises, with 10 of them in the confines of the Mediterranean. It was damaged several times and was even recorded as destroyed, but the men were indeed incredibly fortunate. On one occasion they were attacked by the British submarine *Ultimatum* under Lt-Cdr W. H. Kett, but although Kett reported his quarry as having sunk, *U73* slipped into Toulon just a few hours later without significant damage.

While on the subject of landing agents on the African continent, it may be appropriate to mention that three other men were landed there, but not by U-boat. The 35-ton sailing yacht *Kyloe*, under command of Christian Nissen, a prewar ocean yachtsman, landed Robby Leibbrandt in June 1941 near Port Nolloth in South Africa. Leibbrandt had been born in the Transvaal and had made quite a name for himself as a boxer before participating in the 1936 Olympic Games and falling under the spell of National Socialism while in Berlin.

During the following year a similar yacht, the *Passim* under command of Heinrich Gabers, also a prewar ocean yachtsman, landed two agents on the desolate coast of the Namibian desert and a single man near Mossamedes in Angola, who was captured shortly after arrival there. The other two disappeared, together with their radio transmitter, never to be heard of again. Either they vanished to start a new life or their bleached bones could still adorn that sparsely inhabited and naturally hostile land.

The crews for these yachts were not recruited by the navy but employed directly by the Abwehr. In all cases, they made their way south and back again without putting into port, or indeed without sighting inhabited land. They passed close to the uninhabited island of Trinidade because it was conveniently situated along their route and served as a means of confirming their astronomical navigation. This mysterious island, some 1,500km east of Brazil, is also reputed to have accommodated a secret U-boat base. However, had that story been true then one wonders why these yachts did not use the facilities. After all, the availability of a replenishment port would have made such long voyages in small yachts far safer and more bearable. It may be of interest to add that Heinrich Gabers made two further voyages with *Passim* to land agents in South America.

U331 under Freiherr Hans-Diedrich von Tiesenhausen probably made one of the most determined landfalls in occupied territory, making it difficult to explain why the mission, in November 1941, ended in such unqualified disaster.

The plan was to land a squad of specially trained commandos to blow up the coastal railway running west from Alexandria in Egypt, a vital supply route for the British forces which were then locked in battle with Rommel's Afrika Korps in Libya. Despite the coastal strip being more densely populated than the interior of the desert, the vast stretches of emptiness were impossible to guard and ideal for a surprise attack. Since the rail line lay only a short distance inland, this was a reasonably simple matter of landing, setting up explosives with a pressure trigger and departing again, for the next passing train to detonate its own devastating reception.

However, a two-man patrol of British soldiers approached the landing site, where the footsteps left by the ten-man attack party were easily discovered, but both soldiers were killed silently by a commando and the rower from *U81* left guarding the dinghy. Unfortunately for the Germans, it would seem that the absence of their victims was noticed and a search party dispatched to find why the two sentries had been delayed. This well-armed group ran into the rest of the demolition party a short while after their dinghy had overturned. Dripping wet and cold, the bedraggled bunch were overpowered to be made prisoners of war.

Although it might seem that simply by keeping quiet until the next train passed the attackers would achieve their mission, the British guessed the reason for the intrusion. The Germans decided therefore to tell their captors what had happened, especially as it was suggested that their imprisonment could be made a little easier if the exact location of the explosives was revealed. This hardly involved the disclosing of any great secrets because disturbances in the sandy ground would in any case soon have led the British to the spot before a train would have been allowed to pass.

MUNITIONS TRANSPORTER FOR ROMMEL'S ARMY

U380 was one of those almost unknown boats which hardly features in any account of the war, yet had her life history been conceived as a work of fiction then the critics would probably say that it was too far-fetched.

U380's commander, Kptlt Josef Röther, was 36 years old when he commissioned the boat in Kiel on 22 December 1941, making him older than most submariners. He had transferred from the relative safety first of a netlayer and later a post as chief of the port flotilla in Oslo, to join *U552* under Kptlt Erich Topp as trainee commander. The maturity of his added years gave the men of *U380* the added advantage of having a commander who was prepared to go a considerable way to make life comfortable. His actions were fierce and decisive, but for most of the time he saw no reason to sharpen his crew's responses further than the limitations of the machinery and this attitude helped to create the image of Röther being the daddy of the outfit. He was approachable and never demanded the silliness which many other captains insisted on.

U380 left Kiel during the summer of 1942, called at Trondheim in Norway, and then set course for the bitterness of the Atlantic. The successful period in American waters, often called the Second Happy Time, had already come to an end and everybody on board knew that they were going to face a hard nut in the shipping lanes of the mid-Atlantic. It was not easy, but the boat survived to be refitted in St Nazaire before heading west for another agonising tour. This time things were different. *U380* had hardly crossed the Bay of Biscay when Röther ordered a southerly course and then announced that they were on their way to the Mediterranean. The men instantly recognised that their prolonged kitting out for a long voyage of more than three months had been a blind to mislead possible secret agents along the French coast. At the same time, they also knew that they were going to be exceedingly lucky if they ever touched dry land again.

That famous incident, which has been vividly reconstructed at the end of the film *Das Boot*, where *U96*, under Heinrich Lehmann-Willenbrock, failed to break through the Strait of Gibraltar, had taken place almost exactly a year earlier. By now everybody in the German navy knew of the dangers posed by those narrow, clear waters. The remarkable part of this highly risky undertaking was that *U380* not only got through but also scored an incredible victory. A short while after having established that they had definitely passed through the constricting strait, the men met a massive troop transport. The 11,069grt SS *Nieuw Zeeland*, was sailing under her original Dutch flag, but in British service, when two well-aimed torpedoes sent her to the bottom. The men in *U380* could not believe their luck. Not only had they sunk a valuable target but there were no escorts to harass them. By contrast, a year

The lighthouse at Jandia,
Canary Islands, as it is today.

earlier, when *U81* under Friedrich Guggenberger had sunk the aircraft carrier *Ark Royal* not very far away, he and his men had to endure an incredibly long chase during which over 100 depth charges were dropped.

U380 came from the coldness of a damp autumn into the relative warmth of a Mediterranean winter and life could not have been better for her crew. On 19 November 1942, after a voyage of only two weeks, they put in to the northern Italian port of La Spezia to be confronted with novelties and luxuries they had not even dreamt of. The passage had been so short that a massive Swiss Emmental cheese, which had to be cut down in size because it was too huge for the hatches, was still being used as a seat in the bow torpedo room and could be handed back to the quartermaster uneaten, although in smaller pieces. Emptying the boat was hard work, but necessary to ensure that the interior was cleaned before the next voyage.

The situation on the land battle fronts did not look too good when *U380* left La Spezia on 5 May 1943 for another of the mundane patrols which had occupied the previous months, though the bitterness of all-out war still appeared to be a long way off from the relatively calm waters of the northern Mediterranean, so placid that *U380* could almost operate in a pleasure cruise atmosphere. Two extra men were allowed on the top of conning tower for smoking and another two smoked in the conning tower where a water bucket was located so that cigarettes could be extinguished quickly in the unlikely event of an attack. The coastal waters were relatively free from surprises because the Allied air forces did not mount regular patrols so far away from their main areas of operations.

Above: Kptlt Freiherr Hans-Diedrich von Tiesenhausen stepping ashore while sporting his boat-made Knight's Cross. Some sources have suggested that this was awarded immediately he put in to port after sinking the battleship HMS *Barham*, but this is not correct. He put to sea again on 14 January 1942 and the highly coveted award was not made until the 27th, almost a fortnight later. That would suggest this photograph was taken when he came back to La Spezia on 28 February 1942. He would hardly have received the Knight's Cross as a result of his performance during this voyage: *U331* became stuck in soft mud and had to jettison a number of torpedoes to reduce weight before pulling herself free. *U331's* attempt to blow up the railway line to the west of Alexandria took place some three months before this photograph was taken.

The first clue that something unusual was stirring soon arrived. The boat had not gone very far when a strange instruction arrived that the radio room was to be kept fully manned, even when the boat was made fast in port. By that time, everybody knew that their destination was Livorno (Leghorn), just a few hours away, but no one, not even the commander, had any inkling why they had been ordered there. The boat had never been there before and, in any case, it was not even a naval base but a main trading centre. What was more, the navigator did not have the necessary detailed charts and, when they arrived shortly before nightfall, no one could tell them where to berth.

Livorno could have been one of those dreamy harbours seen in prewar pictures. There was no sign of urgency nor anyone who showed the slightest interest in the arrival of a German U-boat and it took a while before Röther was told to make fast at an out-of-the-way oiling pier. Having done that, the U-boat Command added to the mystery by sending a signal saying that U380 was not to be loaded. It appeared as if no one in the operations room was aware that the boat was already fully laden for a lengthy operational cruise. The reason for this was that domestic arrangements such as providing supplies and looking after the welfare of crews was carried out by U-boat flotilla staff while the operations room, often located some distance from the port, concentrated on the war at sea.

A short while later all became clear. Röther was ordered to unload and remove everything he could spare. All but two torpedoes were to be handed back and, most surprisingly, the larger guns were removed as well to reduce weight. In addition to this, about half the crew were to stay behind in Italy. U380 was to be loaded with as much ammunition as it could carry, to help the retreating army in North Africa. Apparently the Afrika Korps was in a worse state than the public radio announcements had led people to believe.

Although all this can be written very quickly, the men were faced with a torturous task. The sun beat down from a brilliant blue sky, making the interior incredibly hot, and the instructions came in such a scrambled order that men were removing torpedoes from the bottom of the boat, while still trying to find space elsewhere for the food that was carefully stacked on top of them. This had hardly been accomplished when things became even more frantic. Now much of the food was unloaded as well to make room for more ammunition. The pace was so fast that a good number of things went overboard into the water, because it would have taken too long to wait for cranes. The men took it all in good heart. They realised the situation in North Africa had become so chaotic that no one knew exactly what was going on and it was a case of doing everything they could to help comrades on land.

When the commander asked for volunteers to stay behind, not a single man stepped forward. Despite seeing their boat turned into a floating powder keg, no one had the urge to escape the potential disaster and Röther was left with no alternative other than to make the difficult selection himself. After announcing his choice, he went through the boat consoling a number of tearful men who had been ordered to remain behind. 'It is hard enough to make these decisions,' he told them, 'so please do not make it any more difficult for me.'

On Friday 7 May 1943, the sun was already rising into another brilliant clear blue sky when the floating powder keg was carefully trimmed while heading south for Tunis. U380 had not got very far when the U-boat Command in Italy signalled that the city had fallen to the British Army and details of an alternative disembarkation port would be provided as

Above: KptIt Josef Röther came to U-boats in 1941. He served as apprentice commander in *U552* under KptIt Erich Topp, one of only five U-boat men to have been awarded Swords and Oakleaves to the Knight's Cross. Röther survived the war by being made a staff officer towards the end of 1943 and then becoming a prisoner of war in August 1944, when France was overrun by the advancing Allied armies.

soon as possible. Progress, in any case, was not terribly straightforward. The sighting of many floating mines suggested that someone had anticipated the move and placed some potential obstacles along the path. On top of this, the shallowness of the waters off the African coast made the area difficult to operate in.

Röther continued south, hoping someone would help by issuing a few meaningful orders. These were not long in coming, but the instruction to unload at Kelibia (on the Cape Bon peninsula) was somewhat pointless because U380 did not have a map showing this location. The U-boat Command must have realised this. Soon afterwards the nautical position was sent so that the place could be identified on the naval chart. Lookouts guessed that the number of Red Cross hospital ships seen heading in the opposite direction indicated that U380 was in for some intense activity and this was later confirmed by the muffled sound of gunfire as well as numerous columns of smoke rising along the African coast.

The boat had been at sea for two days when U-boat Command sent instructions to pick up a pilot from Kelibia, who was going to direct U380 to a safe disembarkation point, but all this fell flat. The British advance was moving so fast that the priorities changed dramatically. The men on the top of U380's conning tower were surveying the land ahead, looking for a likely contact point with this pilot, when the radio told them that their cargo had been devalued. There was no longer a German army in North Africa and all the ammunition should be thrown overboard to make room for retreating troops. Bearing in mind that the interior of the boat was as hot as a moderate baking oven and that 25 tons of explosives had to be passed up through hatches in the decks by half of the normal crew, this was an exceptionally gruelling undertaking.

A bottle is being passed around the top of the conning tower of *U380*. KptIt Röther, wearing the white cap, is resting his hand on the top of a ventilation shaft. The fact that none of the men are wearing U-boat badges would suggest that this was the end of their first or second voyage.

For a change, the lookouts had the easier option. Instead of battling with inhospitable natural elements, the four men and duty officer could stand on the top of the conning tower without a great deal of physical exertion. They watched gunners on land taking pot shots at aircraft and even tried communicating with them through a megaphone. The U-boat was approached by a tiny picket boat, but the occupants probably could not be sure which side it was on and quickly withdrew again to the relative safety of the shore.

Later, a German Morse message from the land, saying that the men there had a rowing boat but no oars, suggested there was at least someone of the right nationality to rescue. Unfortunately, Röther was in no position to help. The current and the wind were too powerful for manoeuvring *U380's* inflatables. The exchange of Morse messages was brought to an inconclusive end by the radio telling Röther to expect considerable enemy activity, something he had already discovered for himself. The position was definitely becoming increasingly uncomfortable. With virtually no water under the surfaced boat's keel there was little room for manoeuvre. An Italian torpedo boat offered some indication as to the reason for the mass of garbled messages from land, but this brief signal exchange did not bring in any positive news. No one seemed to know what was going on and there did not appear

Left: Kptlt Röther supervising *U380's* engineering officer, LtsZ Stubbe, cleaning fish for lunch. The large bottles in wire baskets and packed in straw contained distilled water for topping up batteries. More convenient and 'unbreakable' plastic containers had not yet been invented.

Below: The German naval ensign fluttering above *U380*.

to be anyone who cared whether U-boat men had risked their lives to save them.

Despite incredible confusion, and no one giving any helpful orders, Röther made the best out of the situation. Just after midnight, during the first few minutes of 10 May, lookouts heard the unmistakable squeak of oars in rowlocks. Peering into the darkness, with a machine gun at the ready, they made out a small boat carrying four men, Obergefreiter Heinrich Pehn and Gefreiters Hans Handwerk, Ernst Schulz and Hans Renner. All had come from different units and could hardly clarify the confusion. However, they told Röther that there were about 40–50 more men on land, but no one there knew about the U-boat. When the four had first seen it, they thought it was a British submarine and went into hiding. Apparently enemy naval units had been dashing along the coast, adding to the discomforts of retreating troops.

This chaotic night-time searching for troops close to the beaches was interrupted by a destroyer which appeared to be aiming at targets on land without noticing the U-boat, but there was little Röther could do. There was no water under the keel and he was now commanding an empty hulk without weapons. The two remaining torpedoes in the bow tubes could not be fired. The removal of much ballast and heavy ammunition had made the boat dangerously unstable, meaning that a prolonged trim dive was necessary before it was wise to engage in any offensive action. In any case, the destroyer was a little too far away for a straightforward surface attack, so Röther had no choice other than to hope that the surrounding confusion provided sufficient camouflage for his precarious predicament.

The chaos continued throughout the night while the men in U380 made a determined effort to find more evacuees without themselves becoming stuck in shallow water. This tense atmosphere was heightened further by a land battery taking pot shots at the U-boat. Fortunately, the gunners were not too good at aiming at a naval target, but a detonation just 400m away was hair-raising enough and sufficient reason for seeking out the relative safety of deeper water.

The peace of the depths did not last long. Soon the interior was filled with the haunting booming of distant depth charges. New instructions were flooding in such quick succession that they could not be acted upon before a counter-order suggested something totally different. Everybody aboard U380 knew that they were not only in a dangerous hot spot but also among some incomprehensible confusion, which historians would probably never sort out. In fact this commotion was so bad that every eye-witness account is totally different and even the crew of U380 have supplied a number of slightly varying descriptions.

Röther's biggest quandary was whether to leave the area. On the one hand, it was becoming noticeably uncomfortable and noisy, but on the other he realised that he could make the difference between life and death or freedom and imprisonment for many. Therefore, he decided to try to remain undetected in an area from where he could still quickly reach any part of the Tunisian coast, hoping the operations room would supply a position from which he could fulfil his objective of rescuing survivors from the depleted German army. In the end, though, he was told that the situation was pointless and that he should make his way back to La Spezia. Going back along the same shortest way he had come was not advisable on account of the abundance of mines which had by now been reported in the area. So it was a case of going the long way around Sicily and creeping north along the shelter of the Italian coast.

The U-boat Command agreed that Röther had been faced with an exceptionally difficult operation during which there were constant changes in situation, but that he and his men had done exceptionally well. The note at the end of U380's log acknowledged that numerous minefields, enemy aircraft, an abundance of naval forces and the confused situation meant that the boat had constantly been at battle stations. The commander and men remained cheerful and efficient which deserves full recognition but it is sad that only four men were rescued as a result of this mammoth undertaking.

Below: U380's emblem, a lucky four-leaved clover, in the U-Boot-Archiv in Germany. Shortly before putting out to sea for the first time, one of the sailors slipped on the grass with all his kit while making his way down to the boat. Lying on the ground he noticed a four-leaved clover, picked it up and took it along as a lucky charm. It was pressed, then framed and later attached to the inside of the conning tower.

Left: A close-up of the badge seen at the edge of the previous picture.

Right: A memorial board for *U380*, compiled after a reunion in 1982.

Above: Table flags from the 3rd to 10th *U380* reunion, now hanging in the U-Boot-Archiv in Germany.

Above: Part of *U380's* corner in the U-Boot-Archiv in Germany. 'We were colleagues. We became friends. Now we are one big family.'

Left: A large four-leaved clover: the emblem of *U380*.

Chapter 7
Neutral Spain

THE SPANISH SUPPLY SYSTEM

Prewar plans for co-operation between Germany and Spain wobbled like a badly balanced yo-yo until 1939 when General Franco brought the matter to an unforeseen conclusion with an open declaration of his country's neutrality. Even so, Germany still hoped to use Spanish naval facilities for supplying surface raiders and submarines and therefore made a concerted effort to build on the foundation laid during the Spanish Civil War when the German had fought on the side of Franco's Nationalists. However, it was not until a few weeks before the beginning of World War 2 that KptzS Hans-Georg von Friedeburg (later Chief of the U-boat Arm's Organisation Department) was instructed to negotiate seriously for permission to create a Spanish-based supply system. No definite conclusions were drawn, but the talks ended with encouraging noises from the Spanish side. Consequently the naval attaché in Madrid, Korvkpt Kurt Meyer-Dröhner, was instructed to prepare plans for using Vigo, Cadiz and El Ferrol as possible German supply bases.

Meyer-Dröhner had been in Spain long enough almost to pass as a national and the contacts he had made now stood him in good stead. Admiral Salvador Moreno Fernandez of the Naval Ministry agreed with the German plans, but emphasised that these could only go ahead as long as foreign authorities did not protest. Once this happened, Spain would want to be seen observing strict neutrality and must take action against Germany. Despite this encouragement, the task set for Meyer-Dröhner was a daunting one. Even Berlin's promise of virtually limitless funds did not ease the major problem of a general shortage of food. There was no way he could acquire the quantities demanded by the High Command, even with the two to four weeks' notice that was the most he was likely to get. The Spanish navy was willing to sell provisions from its own resources, but this could involve information leaking out in unexpected places and at that stage no one could foresee how the rest of the Spanish bureaucracy was likely to react to considerable volumes disappearing into what could turn out to be a bottomless pit.

Eventually, once these proposals were chewed over at ministerial level, co-operation was more forthcoming than Meyer-Dröhner had anticipated from his early discussions, but then the outbreak of war overtook the discussions. In one way this made things a little easier. The German freighters in Spanish ports were likely to remain there because their return routes to Germany had been cut off, and a good number of them already had many of the required supplies on board. Spanish co-operation allowed the Germans to move these around to ensure that they were in the most appropriate locations and, at the same time, the ships were permitted to move to the most advantageous locations within the harbours.

International laws regarding warring nations and non-combatant countries were complex and open to a variety of different interpretations, which probably contributed to there having been very few incidents where warships called in at neutral ports. Among the more famous of such events was the occasion when the pocket battleship *Admiral Graf Spee* made use of the ruling that a warship was allowed into a neutral port for a limited period to seek medical help. Once the period of grace was up, the ship had to leave again or be interned for the duration of hostilities. Merchant ships could remain in such ports, as long as they did not assist the military, and this condition was often enforced by removing their radios to cut them off from their surroundings. Supply ships, even those with civilian crews, were classed as being military and, of course, refuelling a man-of-war or supplying provisions was strictly forbidden. In some cases it was argued that even products such as toothpaste and medical equipment were war goods because they prolonged a ship's ability to fight. All these woolly regulations provided ample scope for deceit, masquerading and hiding vital information from the enemy. For example, who was going to determine the exact length of time allowed for a visit, if the subject was a small submarine and no one saw it arrive?

On the other hand, the outbreak of war also added to the difficulties because the Spanish authorities became more aware of the possible consequences and wanted to make sure that there was no likelihood of them being sucked into the conflict. This nervousness was made considerably worse by the news that British interests were keeping a watchful eye on activities in Spanish harbours. Intelligence suggested that a spy network had been established to ensure that there would be no violation of Spanish neutrality. On top of this, Britain made it clear that any such infringement would result in severe retribution. As a result, at the outbreak of hostilities, General Franco became somewhat reluctant to co-operate with the Germans and started withdrawing his support for their plans. For a short time it looked as if the German preparatory work would be totally frustrated. However, following the rapid conclusion of the Blitzkrieg in Poland, Franco changed his mind once more, allowing the plans to go ahead. This renewed enthusiasm went as far as sending government representatives to various centres of German interest to inform local officials that they should be co-operative.

The acquisition of supplies remained as a major problem and this was now made worse by Franco's system which prevented his possible internal enemies from stockpiling goods for any future conflict against him. For example, one authority controlled all movement of oils and fuels, making it difficult or even impossible for the Germans to collect the quantities required by submarines unless the people running this organisation were going to collaborate. The stockpiling of foodstuffs was eventually solved by buying them in Italy and bringing them over through a civilian transport system for delivery to German naval stores near the ports. All this planning mushroomed into a complicated organisation, occupying significant manpower, out of all proportion to the relatively small quantities it was procuring. Yet, Berlin did not seem to mind and supported the venture with all available resources.

A variety of co-operation schemes had been considered, ranging from the building of German submarines in Spanish shipyards to using Spanish ships to supply both surface raiders and submarines on the high seas, but all this concentrated involvement of a neutral country never progressed beyond the initial planning stages. The war was hardly a few weeks old

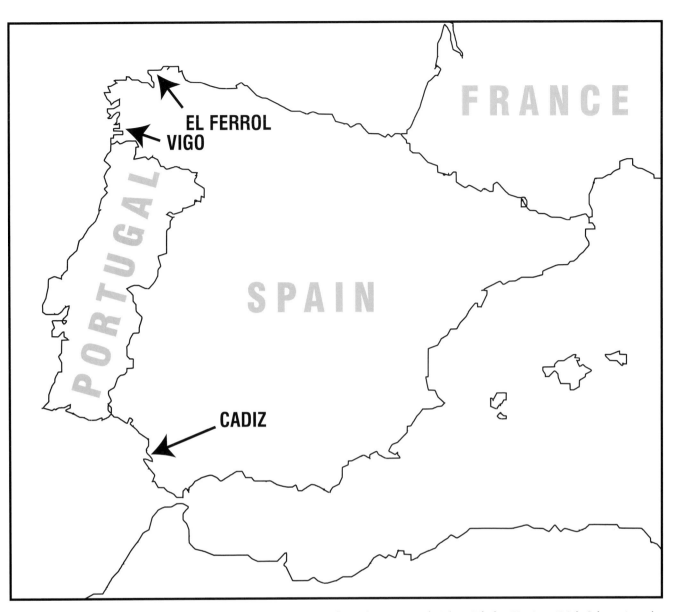

when it became clear that the best Berlin could hope for was for the Spanish authorities to turn a blind eye to German activities. By the autumn of 1939 Meyer-Dröhner's staff had collected together enough provisions to store them as U-boat supply units. These batches consisted of everything a U-boat was likely to need in order to extend its operational period. Since there was no way of taking these out onto the high seas, it became a case of waiting for customers to turn up and collect them. This self-service collection became the linchpin of the entire undertaking. There definitely was no way German or Spanish ships could slip out of harbour to make regular deliveries. What was more, the collectors of the supplies had to call at night without the Spanish authorities officially becoming aware of what was going on. This immediately excluded large surface raiders, but submarines were small and could come and go less obviously. The Germans had to hope that there would be no awkward customers who started asking unnecessary questions. Many vital stages of the operation also rested on the efficiency of single individuals of questionable character delivering the goods at the right time and at the right place. In all, it was a highly precarious and complex operation.

The German freighter *Thalia* (Kapitän Erich Schaper), code-named 'Moro', arrived in Cadiz shortly before Christmas 1939 allowing plans for a refuelling experiment to be put in hand. However, the first boat to try this new system, *U44* (Kptlt Ludwig Mathes), was so short of fuel that the deviation to Spain would not have allowed it to return to Germany if the refuelling failed. Admiral Dönitz did not fancy taking the risk of losing a boat in such a reckless exercise and cancelled the plan, ordering *U25* (Kptlt Viktor Schütze) to go instead.

It turned out to be a tense evening for everybody on the Spanish side. The Naval High Command in Berlin even sent a special observer, Karl Martens. The naval attaché's staff was there as well, making copious notes, so that any faults could be rectified before the next refuelling took place. The problems appeared to be immense but finally it was the unexpected simplicity which threatened to ruin the entire undertaking. Schütze arrived several hours ahead of schedule.

Viktor Schütze (who must not be confused with Herbert-Viktor Schütze of *U605*) joined the navy in 1925 and became one of the first U-boat commanders of the Third Reich. Viktor took over *U25* only two days after the declaration of war, but

Left: U31 (Type VIIA) in Cadiz during the Spanish Civil War with the black, white and red stripes of the old Weimar Republic as identification mark on the front of the conning tower. The boat was commissioned by Rolf Dau on 28 December 1936 and commanded by him until June 1938, when he was replaced by Johannes Habekost. After commissioning U42 during the following month, Dau was fortunate to survive when this large Type IXA became the fourth boat of the war to be sunk, making him the third U-boat commander to become a prisoner of war. Habekost was killed in March 1940, together with the rest of his crew, when U31 was sunk by a Blenheim bomber (Squadron Leader M. Delap) in the shallow channel outside Wilhelmshaven. The boat was later raised and sunk a second time in November 1940 to the northwest of Ireland.

Above: U31 in Cadiz during the Spanish Civil War with what almost looks like the black ghost of a priest, but he was a real person. The gun on this Type VIIA was an 88mm primarily for use against surface targets. It could be elevated to aim at aircraft, but was somewhat clumsy and slow, making it virtually impossible to hit fast moving targets.

with his experience it did not take long to integrate himself and a few other new faces among the crew. To everybody's surprise, he turned up next to the *Thalia* shortly before 20.00hrs on 30 January 1940, when there was still considerable activity in the harbour and the men aboard were not expecting a caller until much later. The lookouts aboard the supply ship did not even see the U-boat approach as it slid in with its upper deck level with the water and only the conning tower showing above it. Fenders were not out yet, meaning the men aboard the *Thalia* had to be quick just to make the U-boat fast safely. An annoying wind and a heavy swell meant it took almost half an hour before *U25* eventually berthed next to the supply ship. Everything went exceptionally smoothly after this and, in less than six hours, *U25* was back on her way out to sea, vanishing into the black night as quickly as she had appeared.

Following this, refuelling in Spanish harbours was whittled down to a fine art and almost became part of the routine. There was certainly very little hassle with the early ventures. Things slowed down somewhat as a result of the incident on 16 February 1940 when the German supply ship *Altmark* was attacked and boarded in Norway by men from the British destroyer *Cossack*. The accidental sinking of the 2,140grt Spanish freighter *Banderas* near Cape Villano by *U53* (Korvkpt Harald Grosse) also resulted in some repercussions. It was 18/19 June 1940 before another attempt was made to refuel in Spain. This time *U43* (Kptlt Wilhelm Ambrosius) took fuel from the freighter *Bessel* in Vigo. The whole operation was completed in four hours without any signs of trouble. By this time, the war situation had changed radically, with Germany now about to take control of the French Atlantic ports. Refuelling in Spanish harbours was no longer likely to be so useful but the facilities there were kept for emergencies and to facilitate some long-range operations into the southern reaches of the Atlantic.

Things did not become uncomfortable until the following year when Britain penetrated deeply into the U-boat code and became aware of what was going on. In fact there were occasions when the Admiralty knew of refuelling operations but did not take action for fear of compromising the fact that Germany's secret radio codes had been breached. On 21 July 1941, for example, *U109* (Kptlt Heinrich 'Ajax' Bleichrodt) was put on tenterhooks following a refuelling from *Thalia* in Cadiz. Although *U109* departed with a good two to three hours of darkness left. By the time the sun appeared over the brilliantly clear eastern horizon, an irritating fishing boat, flying a Spanish flag, still following at a respectful distance, had not been thrown off by several drastic changes in course. Bleichrodt eventually became so fed up with the stool pigeon that he ordered his anti-aircraft gun to be fired over the head of the offender. This discouraged the follower, but not the nasty taste in Bleichrodt's mouth, thinking he had been pursued by the British secret service. The idea of sinking the fishing boat had occurred, but such drastic action could have backfired and produced complicated repercussions.

Worse was to follow three months later. *U564* (Korvettenkapitän [Korvkpt] Reinhard Suhren) refuelled from the *Thalia* in Cadiz during the night of 14/15 October 1941 without too much trouble, but the following night, when *U204* (Kptlt Walter Kell) had made fast, the entire harbour was suddenly illuminated by bright starshells. This did not prevent the refuelling, but it cut things short and the boat retreated before the situation became too hot. Since no signs of retribution followed, it would seem highly probable that the U-boat was not discovered. It seems fairly certain that the perpetrator knew it was there, but not the exact location, and

Above: Probably *U96* under Kptlt Heinrich Lehmann-Willenbrock, one of the first boats to refuel in Spain.

finding a small submarine among harbour clutter was not easy at the best of times. At night, the stark shadows produced by the bright starshells could have hidden an entire flotilla of submarines without an eager inspector at close range being aware that they were there.

Positive evidence of U-boats being refuelled in Spain did not arrive on the British side until the latter days of December 1941, when *U434* (Kptlt Wolfgang Heyda) and *U574* (ObltzS Dietrich Gengelbach) were sunk a few days after having refuelled from the *Bessel* in Vigo. *U434* was attacked by the destroyers HMS *Stanley* (Lt-Cdr D. B. Swan) and HMS *Blankney* (Lt M. V. Thorburn). Almost 50 depth charges were dropped, forcing the U-boat to surface with sufficient damage for the crew to have to scuttle their boat and abandon ship. Forty-two men, including the commander, were rescued.

U574 fared considerably worse, perhaps because Gengelbach succeeded in sinking the *Stanley* with a well-aimed torpedo. He, too, was forced to surface, only to be killed on the bridge by gunfire, while the crew abandoned ship. Scuttling charges had been set and the sloop HMS *Stork* (Cdr F. J. Walker) hit the U-boat with a glancing blow before a final set of depth charges was dropped.

Records in the U-Boot-Archiv state that every man except the commander left the boat and that the attacking warship passed over the sinking spot before disappearing. Returning about 15 to 20min later, the area was illuminated with searchlights and guns were shot in that direction which resulted in the survivors in the water swimming away as fast as they could. Consequently, they

Above: U760 under ObltzS Otto-Ulrich Blum moored by the side of the Spanish cruiser *Navarra* in Spain.

Above: U573, a Type VIIC commanded by Kptlt Heinrich Heinsohn. The boat was damaged by a Hudson bomber near Algiers, but managed to cross the Mediterranean and put in to Cartagena for repairs where it was prevented from leaving again and the crew interned. *U573* was later sold to Spain to serve as *G7* until 1970. Heinsohn and some of his men made their way back to Germany. He was killed in May 1943 as commander of *U438*.

lost touch with each other. An hour or so later, a different ship appeared to rescue a few men. While doing this, it became apparent that there were a number of corpses floating in their life-jackets. Later it became known that the first ship had also picked up a few men, bringing the total number of survivors to 16. It would appear that five men swimming in the water were killed when HMS *Stork* had collided with another ship, HMS *Deptford*, in the confusion of the sinking.

It was not long before skilled interrogators extracted the unquestionable evidence that both boats had been refuelled in Spain. As a result, the British government made diplomatic protests to Spain, bringing further supply operations to a grinding halt for a while. This time, the Spanish reaction was so severe that the German ships in the harbours had guards placed near them to observe virtually every movement and to check who and what went on board. The flow of provisions was effectively halted and there was nothing Germany could do, other than hope that things cooled off. Strict neutrality had become the order of the day.

REPAIRED IN SPAIN

These events did not put a stop to U-boat visits. *U105* was one boat which subsequently sought refuge in Spain. Her first commander, Kptlt Georg Schewe, was promoted to Admiralty Staff Officer with the Flag Officer for U-boats in the Mediterranean and Korvkpt Heinrich Schuch took over in January 1942 for the boat's fifth operational voyage. This cruise was cut short when he was ordered into a deviation to pick up about 80 survivors from the German blockade runner *Spreewald*, which had been accidentally sunk by *U333* under the very highly regarded Kptlt 'Ali' Cremer. Following this, *U105* crossed the Atlantic for a successful cruise in American waters.

Above: Loading stores into a U-boat was a long-winded operation because crates took up too much room and therefore had to be unpacked before the contents were brought on board. This was not so much of a problem when supplying a homeward-bound boat, but still every container had to fit through the narrow submarine hatches. What is more, great care had to be taken so that heavy crates did not end up being stacked on top of soft supplies such as fresh fruit.

Returning then to Lorient in April 1942, Schuch set out again on 7 June for another strike against the United States. This time things did not go too well. He had just crossed the dangerous Bay of Biscay by taking a southerly route, with the hope of avoiding the increasingly dangerous Allied aircraft patrols, when *U105* was none the less surprised by a Sunderland, piloted by Flight Lieutenant E. B. Martin.

It was 09.00hrs when the aircraft dropped out of low cumulus clouds at a range of under a kilometre. The lookout covering that sector was a young lad on his first voyage and Schuch had taken the wise precaution of overlapping his area with two experienced men on both sides, but despite this, the warning was only given slowly. One might wonder at the significance of it being the lookout's first trip and what this has to do with spotting aircraft. After all, the man could see as well as the others who had several voyages behind them. But it must be remembered that he was standing on a 76-metre-long piece of steel, constantly tossing and pitching on restless water and it is quite likely that he felt seasick, homesick, warsick and navysick, none of which would improve his concentration.

Being down below when the watch officer ordered 'Alarm', Schuch reached the bottom of the ladder in the central control room in time to hear the hatch being slammed shut. The confusion of men racing to their diving stations and the deafening shrill of the alarm bells all added valuable seconds to the time it took for the watch officer to make his report. He had hardly collected himself by Schuch's side when three detonations put paid to any form of conversation. Bodies were thrown against steel, the lights went out and stark torch beams cut through the darkness while the engineering officer struggled to maintain control. Instantly Schuch realised that his watch officer had made a mistake by diving. The aircraft was already too close and it would have been better to drive the diesels to top speed in order to try to dodge the depth charges using their superior surface speed.

Breakage reports were not only slow in coming but could hardly be heard above moans and groans flooding out of the blackness. Since emergency lighting failed, those stark torch beams were used to find the powerful spray of water irrigating the control room. Not knowing how deep they were or what was happening to the boat, it was decided to surface again and fend off the attacker with anti-aircraft guns. This was not an entirely satisfactory alternative because the waves were too high for manning the more powerful 37mm on the *Wintergarten* behind the conning tower. Yet, in the dark chaos it seemed better to be disabled on the surface than to allow the boat to drift down into dangerous depths.

Smashed depth gauges made it impossible to tell when the boat was on the surface and a precautionary look through the periscope could waste too much time, but, since it was impossible to open the hatch as long as water pressed down on top of it, it was safe simply to heave at it until it did open. The gun crew for the 20mm weapons followed Schuch to the top. His suspicion had been correct. Waves washing over the lower 37mm anti-aircraft gun made it pointless to bring anyone up to operate it.

At first, as Schuch turned his attention to the still circling aircraft, he could hardly take in his men's reports that the 20mm guns were out of action as well. The ammunition feeder had been torn from one, the end of the barrel had been bent on another and the additional faults hardly mattered. The fact that they would not work in such a precarious situation was the decisive point. Despite his head spinning in pain, Schuch had the feeling that everything was happening in slow motion. Only the aircraft was still moving at its usual speed. There was no response from the diesels. Why was there no increase in speed? The boat was a sitting duck. They could not shoot back. Death was looming terribly close, but there was a chance. Consequently, the alarm bells shrilled again and *U105* dropped once more into the depths.

This proved not to be a terribly good move. Quickly it became apparent that the earlier shower in the central control room had developed into a raging storm, which was now threatening to pull the boat too deep. To make matters worse, it was impossible to find the source of the intrusion. It had to be somewhere behind the mass of provisions stacked around the outside of the compartment and these had been placed there so well that they were not being budged by the encroaching force. Debate was not necessary; there was no alternative to the emergency surfacing procedure of blowing the tanks and using every available pump to empty the filling bilges.

The circling Sunderland was still there, but kept at bay with a number of machine pistols, while every frantic effort was made to repair the larger calibre weapons. Slightly bent barrels meant that aiming was not terribly good, but the men in the aircraft did not know that and kept a respectful distance. Luckily for *U105*, a shortage of fuel finally forced them to break off the action.

Yet, despite being left in peace, it was obvious that *U105* was in a most precarious predicament. Water had entered the boat in such quantities that diving was out of the question and it even looked doubtful whether the boat would remain on the surface for any length of time. The bows were so low that waves constantly washed over the foredeck, forcing the top of the conning tower deep into the raging sea. There was nothing for it other than to send a distress call and ask permission to make for Spain, which was only some 200km to the east. Unfortunately, the engine room was also pretty deep in water and only one of the diesels could be got to work at slow speed. When the Sunderland left, Schuch had first turned on a homeward-bound course, but now, without waiting for instructions, he changed direction to make for the Spanish mainland.

Schuch took several deep breaths while he tried to digest the damage reports flooding in from all quarters. Prospects did not look promising. The provisions in the central control room were removed to reveal a massive metre-long gash in the pressure hull. The munitions chamber below the radio room was flooded and the other failures were so considerable that it would have been better to report what was left working, rather than listing the faults. There was certainly no way the diesels were going to get back to France and now it was even becoming doubtful whether they could cover the relatively short distance to Spain. However, by going in that direction, they would at least reduce the distance they had to swim. It was a case of getting ready to abandon ship while hoping that the Royal Air Force would leave them alone long enough to carry out some vital emergency repairs. This hope was indeed pretty slim. Everybody on the German side knew that the air war had intensified dramatically and there would be no let-up. Another aircraft would soon follow to finish the demolition job started by the Sunderland.

Despite the anguish, injuries and severe damage, *U105* was left in peace to churn slowly eastwards towards neutral Spain. Nothing interfered with progress, the lookouts did not spot anything and the afternoon brought a welcome radio signal that the Spanish destroyer *Melilla* was lying ready in El Ferrol to provide assistance during the last stages of the voyage, if necessary. Although this took a considerable weight off Schuch's mind, he refrained from answering. He did not want to broadcast his position and intentions until shrouded in darkness, when there was less likelihood of the Royal Air Force finding him.

Although some form of normality returned to the life in *U105*, secret documents together with sensitive technical material were placed in their weighted sacks and dropped overboard. Only the emergency cipher pad remained in case further transmissions had to be made. Progress was slow, but there was no interference from the Royal Air Force. Shortly after first light a tug appeared to lead the way into El Ferrol harbour. It quickly became obvious that diplomatic channels had been busy. When *U105* docked by the side of the destroyer *Almirante Antequere*, a German agent, Herr Brendel, and the adjutant of the commanding officer of the naval arsenal, Fregkpt José Ragel, were waiting to come on board for an assessment of what assistance was likely to be required. The welcome could not have been more friendly. Work was quickly put in hand while the men were lodged aboard the *Canarias*, an accommodation ship lying in the harbour. At the same time a number of naval officials appeared to commiserate and to make life as comfortable as possible for the visitors.

Dry dock accommodation was fully occupied and a Spanish cruiser had to be withdrawn to make space for the U-boat, but this happened very rapidly before the end of the day. British interests appeared to have failed to notice the U-boat's presence. Work continued at an almost leisurely pace. None of the Spaniards seemed to show any signs of urgency, making the men from *U105* think their presence was regarded very much as a plus point rather than a potential embarrassment. Things went exceedingly well until five days after the attack by the Sunderland, when a British reconnaissance aircraft, probably a Hampden, was engaged by Spanish anti-aircraft gunners. This performance was repeated the following afternoon, when another aircraft swept low over the U-boat. Had the British discovered *U105* lying secretly in a neutral port? Schuch was becoming impatient. Despite the splendid hospitality, he did not fancy the prospects of an internment camp, especially now that things were looking pretty good for returning to France under the boat's own power. Despite his anguish, nothing stirred on the diplomatic front. Yet the British reconnaissance flights continued. Schuch was told that these were not a regular feature, making him guess that the British were probably aware of the U-boat's presence and were waiting for it to move out into international waters. The thought of sitting in a mousetrap as bait did not appeal.

On this occasion, co-operation with the Luftwaffe brought such fruitful results that *U105* was provided with air cover for the return journey to France. The plan was for the *Melilla* to escort *U105* beyond the three mile limit where a Ju-88 would take over. This actually worked. There, at the appointed time, appeared a solitary bull-nosed Junkers to circle around the slowly moving U-boat, as it plodded back along the last leg of the journey. At one stage a Sunderland appeared, but either it was put off by the heavy fighter or was too low on fuel. Whatever, it did not attack, nor summon reinforcements, allowing *U105* to make fast in Lorient on 30 June after a passage lasting two terribly long days.

U105 was not the only boat to creep into El Ferrol for emergency repairs. *U193* (Korvkpt Hans Pauckstadt) was damaged in the Bay of Biscay on 9 February 1944 and put in to El Ferrol the following day, to leave again two weeks later and successfully reach Lorient on 24 February 1944.

INTERNED IN SPAIN

The summer of 1943 saw the Atlantic become exceptionally precarious for U-boats. Over 40 boats were lost during May. The figures for June did not look quite so bleak but only because U-boats had temporarily been withdrawn from the most troubled waters, but July saw almost 40 boats go down. So when *U760* (Kptlt Otto-Ulrich Blum) and *U262* (Kptlt Heinz Franke) left La Pallice on 24 July, everybody on board must have known that there were exceptionally high chances of them featuring in these shattering loss statistics. The only consolation was that neither boat was going into the dangerous waters of the North Atlantic. They were heading west, along the great circle and the shortest route to Cape Hatteras in North Carolina where both commanders were to be free to exploit whatever opportunities were on offer.

In the first days of the voyage *U760* successfully avoided a confrontation with aircraft and even inspected a neutral Swedish freighter, the 6,584grt SS *Bali*, but then the U-boat Command signalled an order that *U760* was to top up her fuel tanks from *U664* under Kptlt Adolf Gräf. This unscheduled opportunity had been created by an attack which was forcing Gräf back to base. Since he had left Brest only three days before *U760*, this clearly underlined the dangers of crossing the Atlantic, even while trying to avoid confrontation. A couple of days after the refuelling, the Allied superiority was further

U760 to the south of the Azores during August 1943, only a few days before the devastating attack which forced the boat to seek out repair facilities in Vigo. Although British aircraft had long since become a dangerous threat, *U760* is still equipped with only a single 20mm anti-aircraft gun.

emphasised by the sinking of *U664*. *U760* was living on borrowed time and did not fare much better.

A Liberator swooping down from low cloud on 12 August 1943 placed three depth charges uncomfortably close to her bows. Having seen the bomb bay swing open, the lookouts were numbed by a deafening blast, but were quickly brought back to their senses by a drenching from a massive fountain of cold water. When the commotion subsided they became aware that the boat was running in a tight circle at high speed. No one on the top of the conning tower knew that the rudder had jammed and it took a while before they collected their senses to shout orders down the voice pipe. Finding that there was no response, the men wondered whether everybody else had been killed. Down below, though, things were not as bad as the first inspection made out. There was only one really serious casualty. Obergefreiter Artur Henrich was lying unconscious on the floor of the central control room as a result of having been hit on the head by a magazine for the 20mm anti-aircraft

Above: Another photograph taken during that fateful voyage when *U760* was forced into Vigo for repairs. This was taken about one month earlier, while refuelling from the damaged and therefore homeward-bound *U664*. The first watch officer and Obersteuermann of *U664* were lost overboard while uncoupling the hosepipe a few minutes after this picture was snapped.

U760 seen here in the Baltic after having been rammed by the target ship *Venus*. Although this made a considerable mess of the conning tower, the damage was only superficial and did not impair the diving qualities of the submarine.

gun. The rest were working frantically to repair the damage, despite a large number of injuries.

Meanwhile, the Liberator was still circling, trying to encourage the submarine to dive by shooting at it, but Blum did not dare oblige at first because no one knew whether they were sitting in an iron coffin or a serviceable boat, capable of surfacing again afterwards. Then, amidst all this confusion, the radio operator reported signal transmissions. This made Blum think that the Liberator had probably run out of depth charges and had called in reinforcements. He decided to dive. It was only much later, long after the war, that Blum learned that the aircraft was carrying a new secret weapon in the form of two acoustic torpedoes and diving was just what the Liberator crew wanted the U-boat to do since these were designed to home in only on submerged submarines.

As luck would have it, the men of U760 made a mess of their diving procedure. One of the vents was stuck, causing the boat to plummet exceedingly fast into the depths, so fast that the engineering officer ordered the engines to be cut. Whether it was the absence of noise, or whether the acoustic torpedoes were dropped from too great a height has never been ascertained, but U760 survived.

Below: A rather poor quality but exceedingly rare photograph of the sailing yacht *Kyloe* moored by the side of *U760* with the Spanish cruiser *Navarra* in the background. Yachts like this made several voyages to Ireland, South Africa and South America to land agents. Their captains and crews were not naval personnel, but prewar ocean yachtsmen employed directly by the Abwehr.

Once safely down in the depths, the crew discovered that Matrosengefreiter Günter Werner was not at his post. Somehow he must have been washed overboard during that frightful blast and the chaotic diving manoeuvre. Blum did not hesitate. He turned the boat round, telling his men that no one would be abandoned, no matter how difficult things might get. Sadly, all efforts to find Werner failed. It was now one of those exceptionally black nights when it was impossible to make out the bows and stern from the conning tower and the unfortunate man did not have a light. Eventually the boat crawled away while the men, with heavy hearts, made every effort to restore some form of sanity to what felt like the end of their days.

There were numerous injuries and considerable damage. The engines were definitely not going to keep working as far as America but, fearing another attack, the men needed to distance themselves as quickly as possible from the spot where they had met the Liberator. One of the most pressing problems was the radio. It had been damaged by the blast, making it impossible to report the incident to headquarters. It took a while, but eventually a hastily improvised set was brought up from below, the men rigged up a long wire to the top of the periscope and then the operator started fumbling about underneath a cover of blankets. He needed a lamp, but showing a light was not recommended. The silence dragged into what seemed like eternity, but then the eruption of a loud cheer told everybody that they had been heard. The U-boat Command appeared not to be terribly sympathetic and used the situation to best advantage by directing U760 to refuel U84 (Kptlt Horst Uphoff), a Type VIIC, on its way back from Brazil.

Diving at the rendezvous in order to remain out of trouble enabled the men of U760 to hear the booming of a concerted depth charge barrage. The resonance was felt throughout the boat, suggesting that it was not too far away. It appeared obvious that U84 was having a rough time, but there was nothing anyone could do about it. Even if U760 had been in a fit state, the boat did not have any effective weapons against aircraft and nothing at all with which it had much chance against small manoeuvrable warships such as destroyers or convoy escorts. New acoustic torpedoes were in production, but a few more weeks were required before the first ones were delivered to operational boats. U84 did not make it. The boat was probably sunk on 24 August 1943 by a homing torpedo dropped from an aircraft piloted by Flt Lt W. A. Felter.

Eventually U760 surfaced into an uneasy misty calm to rock gently on the Atlantic swell. Watch officer, LtzS Hanns Parsch, Obergefreiter Anton Agl, Obergefreiter Karl Hafner, Bootsmaat Wilhelm Otten and Obergefreiter Egon Scheil were on duty on the conning tower when a camouflaged superstructure appeared out of a penetrating mist. Parsch did not wait to identify the ship. He and his men crashed down onto the central control room floor, and the boat dropped down under the waves. The whole crew hoped they had not been seen, but it quickly became obvious that they had already been detected. One well-placed detonation followed another and then, suddenly, inexplicably, the propeller noises vanished. The deadly silence remained until after nightfall when U760 surfaced among dark and empty waves. The stench of diesel oil quickly told the lookouts that something was afoot and soon they discovered that one or more of the saddle tanks had been torn open, allowing masses of precious fuel to leak out. Could it have been this which made the destroyer think that it had scored a kill?

Cruising back to base is not the correct description of what followed. Repeated engine failures were now a fact of life, with one or other of the two diesels protesting in turn until emergency repairs coaxed them a little further. The U-boat Command helped by suggesting that *U760* should use the 'Piening Route' through Portuguese and Spanish waters. This was named after Korvkpt Adolf Cornelius Piening of *U155*, who was the first captain to use it to crawl home successfully with a badly damaged boat by sticking close to the Spanish coast. The great advantage lay in the abundance of small fishing boats working the area, which helped to confuse enemy radar.

Sadly for the men in *U760*, it quickly became apparent that this route was not going to help them. By the time land came into sight, it was obvious that the engines where not even going to go as far as the coast and for some time it looked as if the boat would have to be abandoned. However, the radio had now been repaired sufficiently to ask for help and Blum suggested that a Spanish ship might be sent out to tow the boat into the nearest port. Yet, despite having sighted the lighthouse at Oporto (in Portugal, less friendly to the Germans), things did not look too good. Lying on the seabed during the hours of daylight, the men constantly heard one depth charge barrage after another. They were pleased that the detonations were too far away to be a threat to their wrecked boat.

The following night the U-boat Command suggested that *U760* should try to reach Vigo, but that was not so easy. The engines had mutinied. Using a signal pistol, the men managed to draw a couple of fishing boats closer and then used a megaphone and dictionary to request a tow. It worked. After considerable shouting and waving of arms, one of the boats accepted a line and very slowly pulled *U760* into port. Things continued to go well. Making fast by the side of the cruiser *Navarra*, *U760* was visited by a representative of the naval attaché, who even smuggled on board a number of piston rings inside his trouser legs. A flotilla engineer from Lorient turned up to check that the damage was as bad as the men had made out and then things settled down to the usual Spanish pace of not getting too ruffled about unpreventable events. The Germans were well cared for, repairs were put in hand and *U760* was on the verge of departing again when the Spanish authorities withheld permission to leave port. They even sent a diver to lay a chain around the propellers. Things looked gloomy.

U760 had run into Spain at exactly the wrong moment. First an Allied landing craft with about 20 men on board also sought refuge in Spain and the political haggling involving their release resulted in the Germans also being detained. In addition to this, a large number of Italians turned up in several harbours together with their military hardware. Mussolini had fallen from power in July 1943, the day after *U760* had left France. Then there followed the Allied invasion of mainland Italy on 3 September and an armistice between the Allies and the Italian government on the 9th. Consequently a number of Italian warships chose to run to Spain rather than continue the war on the home front against Germany. This massive political upheaval ensured that *U760* did not have an easy time.

Some of the crew were moved to an internment camp near El Ferrol, while others remained as a maintenance team. The Geneva Convention assured that one man, the medical officer, Marinestabsarzt Dr Harald Koch, should be allowed home. The others were made reasonably comfortable. Spanish conversation courses were on offer, there were numerous excursions into the hinterland, men could explore the local bars and the accommodation was quite good. In fact, there was very little to complain about. Living at the expense of the Spanish government was certainly less stressful than surviving in a U-boat. What was more, the internees were joined by survivors from the British cruisers *Glasgow* and *Enterprise* and

later they enjoyed the company of men from *U617* (Korvkpt Albrecht Brandi), which had been beached in northern Africa.

Watch officer Hanns Parsch wrote that he had a terrific time and it is quite likely that the internment saved his life. There were a few little niggling problems. Food for the crew was not always as plentiful and varied as the men would have wished. There was a brief spell of a few days when they lived on an exclusive diet of hazelnuts, but the German community took pity on them and helped to improve matters. They even made arrangements to join a tennis club and enjoy other recreational activities. Life could hardly have been better. Yet, sadly, during one of these activities, Obermaschinistenmaat Wilhelm Arndt was hit and killed by a ricocheting bullet at the rifle range in Vigo on 2 February 1945.

One day, while Hanns Parsch was surveying the scene, he was called to watch a somewhat dilapidated yacht, the *Kyloe*, make fast next to *U760*. Her sunburnt master, Hein Mück, was passed off as a civilian, although in reality he was on the payroll of the Abwehr, having just come back from a cruise to South America where he had landed a secret agent. He had been at sea for too long, had seen too much of the yacht and was pleased to take the very first opportunity of abandoning it, to transfer his men back home to Germany. The skeleton crew of *U760* was pleased. The yacht doubled the size of the German fleet. Its cabins may have been cramped, but they were airy, comfortable and much better than the dark interior of the submarine.

The commander, 'Ole' Blum, even took the opportunity of finding a bride and, with only a short while left before the Third Reich collapsed, married an adopted niece of Admiral Wilhelm Canaris. The men felt pleased when the darkest days of the war were over and the hope of going home arose once more. Sadly, a number of them knew that they no longer had anything to return to. Whatever they had left behind had been destroyed and their families were dead. Consequently some considered joining the Spanish navy, but such dreams failed to materialise and the end of the war resulted in them being imprisoned by Allied forces, after both men and boat were taken to Britain.

U573 (Kptlt Heinrich Heinsohn) was in a similar position to *U760*, but in less turbulent times. Arriving in Cartagena on the Mediterranean coast with considerable damage on 2 May 1942, the crew was interned, but diplomatic channels were flowing well and the boat was sold to Spain, which commissioned it as *G7* and kept it in service until 1970. Once the fuss died down, the men were allowed back to Germany. Although it has often been claimed that *U570* (Kptlt Hans Rahmlow) was the only U-boat to have surrendered to an aircraft, this is false because, in the first instance, *U573* also surrendered to the attacking Hudson of 233 Squadron RAF. However, the aircraft was short of fuel and there were no supporting forces in the vicinity to accept the surrender. Therefore, finding himself alone in an empty sea, Heinsohn took advantage of the situation by repairing his boat and making for neutral Spain. This prolonged his life for almost exactly one year. He returned to Germany to command *U438*, in which he was killed on 6 May 1943.

At least two other crews were interned in Spain, but these arrived without their boats. Both *U566* (Kptlt Hans Hornkohl) and *U966* (ObltzS Eckehard Wolf) were scuttled after a chain of attacks put the boats out of action. The men went ashore in dinghies while others were picked up by fishermen. Despite considerable injuries only eight men from *U966* went missing, while the rest were interned by Spanish authorities. However, supervision was not too tight and possibly nine from *U966* and the entire complement from *U566* made their way back home.

Above: A photograph taken from the Spanish fishing boat *Fina* from Vigo of survivors from *U566* (Kptlt Hans Hornkohl). The boat had been seriously damaged by a Wellington piloted by Flight Sergeant D. Cornish during the previous night and had to be scuttled some 50km west of Oporto because both propellers and steering gear no longer functioned.

Above: Survivors from *U566* in life-rafts, tied together to prevent them from drifting apart, photographed from the Spanish fishing boat *Fina*. The men were taken ashore and later allowed to make their way back to France.

Right: The original caption for this photograph states that this is *U566* after its first operational voyage. Obviously it had a clash with something and survived...

Left:...However, *U566's* first operational voyage ended in Kirkenes (Norway) on 19 August 1941 and that was some time before bunkers were constructed. What is more, there were no such concrete monstrosities in Kirkenes, as can be seen in the background here. *U566* was rammed during a submerged attack on convoy SL119 and made it back to Brest on 5 September 1942. The bunker matches the pattern of the one in Brest pretty well, so this more likely shows the homecoming after a later voyage.

Chapter 8
The Mysterious Canary Islands

WAS THERE A SECRET REFUELLING BASE?

Most of the material about Villa Winter and the 'secret U-boat base' at Jandia on Fuerteventura has appeared in publications where readers could be filled with awe because they were unlikely to know a great deal about submarines nor be in a position to check the authenticity of the stories. The articles also appear to have been aimed at people who were searching for sensationalism rather than hard, factual news. So is there any truth in them?

For readers who are unfamiliar with the legend, the story goes that General Franco gave considerable tracts of land on Fuerteventura to Germans who had helped the Nationalists during the Spanish Civil War. At that time, shortly before the beginning of World War 2, the island was still fairly inaccessible from Europe and, on top of this, it was sparsely inhabited, meaning that there were very few people in a position to interfere with strange buildings. The majority of locals kept clear of the Jandia peninsula because it was also exceedingly difficult to reach from the major towns. Even today, with four-wheel drive and some pretence at road building, large tracts of that land can still be visited only on foot. Much of the terrain is so torturous that competent mountaineers offer it respect and tackle the treacherous slopes with great caution.

Anyone who contemplated building even a small house among that desolation during the 1930s needed a strong commitment to nature, a burning desire to get away from civilisation and considerable sums of money to move the necessary building materials into such an inhospitable region. Gustav Winter seems to have been just such a person. He was a German, a true

Below: The author standing on the main coast road on Fuerteventura, Canary Islands, at the junction with the track leading over the mountains to Cofete, the nearest settlement to Villa Winter. The restaurant advertised on the stone can be recommended.

eccentric, determined to shut himself off from the world. Some time before the beginning of World War 2 he built a massive villa on the lonely northfacing side of the Jandia Mountains. These are the highest peaks on the island and their steep boulder-strewn slopes ensured that he was not likely to receive many visitors. The nearest town, the small fishing port of Morro del Jable, was then several hours' walk away, along a narrow twisting footpath. Even today, when the town has grown into a tourists' metropolis, it still marks the end of the surfaced road. This communication link was nothing more than a dirt track when Villa Winter was built and, at that time, there were only a dozen or so motor vehicles on the entire island. Gustav Winter could not have chosen a more remote location for his large villa. The adjective describing the size needs further emphasis — at the time it was built, the house was probably among the largest on the island.

This much seems to be fact, but the stories then tell us that the house was connected by underground passages to a massive bunker used for refuelling and repairing U-boats. Apparently, the complex was backed up by a couple of airfields and all manner of supporting facilities. The tale of a secret replenishing base was given further circumstantial credence by accounts of Gustav Winter appearing in the markets of Gran Canaria, buying fresh fruit and vegetables for a hundred or so people at a time.

Various accounts about Villa Winter spread across Fuerteventura in the postwar years and the story of the bunker also found an avid readership in European magazines until the availability of hired four-wheel-drive vehicles for the treacherous dirt track made those desolate stretches of the north coast accessible to the more adventurous tourists. When visitors discovered that there was no sign of such a construction, the guardians of the fable changed tack and quickly converted the concrete pens into a natural cave, accessible from the sea by an underwater passage. Though obviously, they explained, the landward access and the tunnels connecting it with Villa Winter were blown up at the end of the war when the Germans had no further use for the installation.

Not long ago, we are told in addition, two divers rediscovered this monstrosity. Making a determined effort, they found an underwater route into the cavern, where they were overwhelmed by the riches to be seen. Not one, but two, then three and later even four U-boats were reported still to be made fast to concrete jetties. Unfortunately, no one has yet tracked down the divers, nor named them, nor come up with the slightest hint of where this massive cave is to be found. A basin large enough to hold four U-boats with space for turning them round must measure at least some 100m x 150m, so this must indeed be an awe-inspiring cavern of frightening proportions. One wonders whether a natural hole of that size could have remained secret, even on the sparsely inhabited slopes of Jandia. It certainly would be a powerful contender for the record books.

Could it then have been a man-made cave? Unfortunately, a man-made hole of that size would have involved such difficult construction through hard rocks as to make the venture highly unlikely. On top of that, there is no evidence of any significant excavations near Villa Winter.

There are, however, several features in the area that might seem to support the story in part. There are a number of large sea caves near the tiny fishing village of Ajuy, close to the old historic capital of Fuerteventura. None of these penetrates deeply into the land but at least one of the bigger caves has been connected to the cliff top by drilling a series of one metre diameter holes. This adds a weird dimension to some slippery steps leading down to the water's edge and a number of 'blind' tunnels, but it would appear that these are industrial relics from the days when lime was burned on the cliffs. The steel-lined shafts leading up from the cave are nothing more than ventilation ducts.

There is also an airstrip on the far western tip of Jandia which has quite likely been there since before World War 2. It was made by flattening the hard yellowish limestone rock and adding a layer of finely ground black basalt. This contrasting colour makes it easy to spot from a distance and the massive runway could well have served as an emergency landing strip in wartime. There is evidence of a number of bigger masts having been there at one time, but no traces of anything to suggest it has ever been used as a base or airport. The suggestion that all this evidence was removed at the end of the war does not really hold water because, for example, sufficient traces remain to reconstruct many of the defensive installations around the south coast of England which were demolished at around the same time.

Even if the airstrip is credited with having been operational, the stories about the Germans flying in supplies for the U-boat base near Villa Winter are still absurd because during the war there was no connection between the two and a team of hundreds of donkeys would have walked for several days over the most difficult terrain to reach one from the other. Nor is there any trace of accommodation or other facilities for the mass of people who would have been required to make all this work.

Since evidence for the base has never been produced, one can conclude that it probably never existed. However, trying to prove that something does not exist is not easy, especially among the higgledy-piggledy isolation of the Jandia shore.

Above: The unsurfaced track to Cofete photographed in 1999. Further up in the mountains it becomes narrow and most precarious, hanging on the side of steep hills with many sharp bends, only just wide enough to take a car. During World War 2 there were hardly any surfaced roads on Fuerteventura and the island had only a handful of motor vehicles.

During the mid-1980s, shortly after Wolfgang Hirschfeld (distinguished historian, author of *A Secret Diary* and *U-boat Radio Operator*) first heard the story of Villa Winter, he accompanied me to find three U-boats hidden in the heart of the Hamburg docks. These could be seen at low tide and had been rotting away in the ruins of an old bunker since the end of the war. The discovery had been accidental, through some documents found among a pile of papers at the Royal Navy's submarine museum (HMS *Dolphin*) in England and was quite sensational at the time. In fact, many authorities did not believe that they were there, even after they had seen the photographs we had taken. Therefore, if three U-boats could remain undetected in such a massive city, it would not be inconceivable for others to be moored in out-of-the-way locations such as the edge of the Fuerteventuran desert.

Despite the presence of such surprises in over-populated Europe, after considering the available information and visiting the northern Jandia shore dominated by Villa Winter, one must come to the conclusion that a secret U-boat base could not have existed there. And one of the type that has been suggested would not have been practical in any case. Bear in mind that most U-boat commanders could not negotiate the Kiel Canal on their own and during the war the authorities demanded that U-boats should pass through the locks there one at a time, although they are big enough for a dozen or so ships of that size, and one can assume that negotiating an underwater tunnel is impossible. This is something which might occur in films or fiction but not in reality. It must also be remembered that Villa Winter is situated on a windward shore with treacherous currents and often forceful waves.

Finally and most conclusively of all, there are no records of any U-boats having used Jandia, and the International Submarine Archive in Germany (U-Boot-Archiv) has never heard of anyone who refuelled there.

Left: Although this looks like debris left from a building site, the rocks are natural. On the left is the type of cart track found on Fuerteventura before the modern road building programme changed the face of the island, making outlying villages accessible to motor transport.

Above: This tanker, photographed on Gozo (Malta), shows the type of vehicles used during World War 2. A fleet of these would have been required to supply fuel for submarines and it seems highly unlikely that the wartime roads of Fuerteventura could have carried them. Several tankers like these would have been required to fill the fresh water tanks of a submarine.

Right: The northern slopes of the Jandia peninsula on Fuerteventura, showing the mountain track leading down to Cofete. The Villa Winter can just be made out as a light spot towards the right.

Above: Villa Winter nestling in splendid isolation at the foot of the Jandia slopes. Morro del Jable, the nearest town with shops, harbour and other facilities, lies on the other side of the 700-metre (2,300ft) high mountains.

Above: A coastal track leading down to the northern shores with Cofete and Villa Winter to the right of the mountains in the far distance. Along this entire length of rugged mountains, there appear to be only two passes from south to north capable of carrying vehicles and it is doubtful whether those tracks would have been substantial enough during World War 2 to allow access for the type of traffic required by a U-boat base. There appear to be no harbour facilities near Cofete. Therefore the unloading of stores from ships would have been most precarious and required a massive army of workers.

Above: A coastal track leading along the northern shores towards Cofete and Villa Winter.

Above: These three metre high waves on the north coast of Fuerteventura were photographed on a day when the south coast was dead calm. Such contrasting conditions appear to be relatively frequent on the island, which makes one wonder why anyone would choose this exposed shore for landing boats.

Above: The author exploring a derelict farm in the mountains near to Villa Winter. These magnificently constructed buildings were made from two dry stone walls with the gap between them filled with sand. They would have been quite comfortable and substantial and there appear to be a fair number of such dwellings, meaning a few people could have been accommodated in the area. However, there are no signs of any communications between them and supporting services, such as water supplies, are missing. Furthermore, the debris left behind suggests that families with small children occupied these lonely settlements, rather than bands of highly trained soldiers.

Above: The volcanic rocks of the Jandia peninsula contain a number of natural caves, but most of them are tiny and would not accommodate more than about half a dozen people. This shows the entrance to one such natural cave.

Above: The mysteriously fascinating larger caverns near Ajuy on the west coast of Fuerteventura. Even these huge natural holes are too small to accommodate boats and the massive banks of boulders near their bases together with waves driving in to the shore would make it highly dangerous to approach them by boat.

Above: The author standing on one of the two runways on the southern shores of the Jandia peninsula. Although looking like sand, the yellow surface is a hard limestone, suitable for carrying heavy weights of aircraft landing or taking off. It seems to have been covered with the finely ground black basalt to make the strip stand out in the barren landscape. During the war, the narrow black-surfaced road in the background would have been nothing more than an unmade track, if it was there at all.

Left: This looks like an improvised roller made from filling an oil drum with concrete, found by the airstrip near Jandia lighthouse. The darker black-basalt-covered runway can be seen in the distance. Villa Winter lies a good day's walk on the other side of the mountains.

Left and below: The runway near the Jandia lighthouse.

Below: Surprisingly there are only a few large wrecks on the Fuerteventuran shores, probably because the sparsely inhabited island was rarely visited by ships of any size. Local fishermen use small craft which can be launched from beaches. None of the wrecks around the island give any indication of them having had a connection with the military and they were more likely to have been cargo carriers or pleasure craft.

U-BOATS ON THE CANARY ISLANDS

Even if the story of a German buying food for a large number of people is true, whether this was Gustav Winter or not, it can be explained by the number of U-boats which are known to have been replenished elsewhere in the Canary Islands. In addition to this, the entire crew of U617 (Fregkpt Kurt Sturm) landed on Gran Canaria, but without their boat.

Refuelling facilities were made possible by various German cargo ships which sought refuge in the Canaries as in other neutral harbours at the beginning of the war. Many of the later clandestine meetings with these hurriedly converted stationary supply ships took place at the Spanish mainland ports as already described, and the following two incidents have been included as examples of replenishment operations which definitely took place in the Canary Islands.

Towards the end of March 1941, U105 under Georg Schewe was supplied in this way to extend its range for a mission into the South Atlantic. Despite this having been supposedly carefully pre-planned, the operation ran into problems but the fact that Schewe was made a knight of the Iron Cross two months later would suggest that he was not the one responsible for the mix-up over the refuelling.

U105 was one of 14 Type IXB boats, which became a highly successful group with several extreme records to their credit. The reason for this was that more experienced commanders were placed in these larger long-distance boats and being able to travel further afield meant they appeared unexpectedly in remote areas where good harvests could be reaped before effective anti-submarine forces were established there.

Less than a week after leaving Lorient in France, while heading south within sight of the Spanish coast, Schewe was told by signal that he was to use the supply ship *Charlotte Schliemann* (known by the code-name 'Corrientes'), which had been interned at Las Palmas in the Canaries and was now being used as a stationary supply base for U-boats. Schewe approached the Canaries according to schedule to within sight of the lighthouse at Ponte Delgada. It was 04.00hrs when the light came into view, meaning there was ample time to take accurate bearings to check the refuelling location for the coming night. Schewe waited until shortly before 02.00hrs the next night for the moon to set, before creeping silently into Las Palmas harbour in full view of houses along the seafront. In those days Las Palmas was a small town and no one on land showed the slightest interest in the submarine, although it was well known that British informers kept an eye on the goings-on. Reaching the *Charlotte Schliemann* was easy. The problem came when Schewe spoke with a mystified crewman who told him the refuelling had been scheduled for the following night. Neither men nor equipment were ready and there was nothing for it other than for U105 to slip out again and wait in deep water until matters could be sorted out.

The misunderstanding left Schewe somewhat red-faced. Rechecking orders, he confirmed the instructions were that the refuelling should take place on the first day of March between 01.00 and 05.00hrs. Counting back in the diary to see that they had not accidentally lost a day, he established that it was indeed 02.00hrs on 1 March and it was not a leap year either. It would seem that somewhere along the administrative line was a person who took the night of 1 March to start at the end of the day and discounted the first few hours from midnight until daylight. It obviously was one of those gremlins of which the German navy had a good number and there was

nothing anyone in U105 could do about it, other than grit their teeth, shrug their shoulders and wait on the seabed off Gran Canaria.

Darkness had hardly fallen on the next night when another signal told Schewe that the schedule had been changed. U124 (Georg-Wilhelm Schultz) was to go into Las Palmas on 3 March, U105 on the 4th and U106 (Jürgen Oesten) during the following night on the 5th. The men aboard *Charlotte Schliemann* were going to be busy. At the same time the waiting boats were told to patrol the western areas off the Canary Islands, where they might run into shipping, but U105 did not spot anything. Everything was calm without any significant activity.

March 4 was not yet an hour old when U105 was made fast on the seaward side of the supply ship. High waves being blown directly into the harbour made the situation rather tricky because a Swedish ship had anchored close to the more convenient landward side. However, this time everything went well, although the U-boat was constantly battered against the larger hull, though the well-padded fenders prevented too much damage being done. A hose was brought down, crates of fresh provisions were handed over and there was time for some men to have showers. Shortly before the first signs of daylight streaked across the far eastern horizon, U105 headed out to sea again, dived for testing the trim and then continued southwards on the surface.

Three months later, when U69 under Jost Metzler called in on the Canary Islands, it was not a pre-planned operation but as a result of considerable desperation caused by the wiping out of much of the German supply fleet. Nine surface ships had been distributed over unfrequented parts of the ocean to coincide with the breakout of the battleship *Bismarck* and the heavy cruiser *Prinz Eugen*. However, U110 under Fritz-Julius Lemp had been captured a couple of weeks earlier together with all its secrets. Consequently Britain gained a valuable insight into the U-boat radio code and dispatched warships to reduce the size of Germany's supply system.

U69 was the first Type VIIC boat to be launched and would normally not have operated as far south as the Nigerian and Ghanaian coast. However, Admiral Dönitz was already famous for exploiting every opportunity, and the presence of such an unusually large supply fleet provided the impetus to take the U-boat war into far-flung areas where rich pickings could be expected. Jost Metzler was the type who could be trusted with any impossible mission, though he came over as an easy-going, almost sluggish type of person who never seemed to be alarmed about anything. The reason for this was that he had put considerable effort into the training of his crew and he knew his men could be relied upon to do their bit whenever it came to the crunch. His system functioned like well-oiled clockwork, therefore there was no need to get excited or bully the men in times of an emergency.

U69 left France on 5 May 1941, three weeks before the sinking of the battleship *Bismarck*, to be refuelled from the supply ship *Egerland* near the Canary Islands before venturing into the shipping lanes around St Paul's Rock in the central Atlantic near the Equator. From there Metzler sailed to Lagos (Nigeria) where mines were laid in the harbour approaches. Another set of mines was deposited off Takoradi (Ghana) before he made his way back to Accra (Ghana) where the 5,444grt motor vessel *Sangara* was torpedoed and sunk inside the harbour. All these operations took place in exceptionally shallow water; so shallow that at one stage there was only one metre of water below the keel. Being in such a position was

Above: U69 under Kptlt Jost Metzler with men using the open-air washroom on the upper deck while cruising in the tropical waters to the south of the Canary Islands. In the foreground is a 88mm quick firing gun and the circular intake for the radio aerial is clearly visible above the wave deflector on the front of the tower

somewhat uncomfortable, especially as coastal currents and tides could easily add a catastrophic dimension to the undertaking. Therefore Metzler quickly turned the boat round to seek out greater depths. *Bismarck* had been sunk by this time and the Royal Navy was hitting hard at the supply ships. First, the *Egerland* disappeared and then the other southern ship, the *Lothringen* was sunk by the cruiser HMS *Dunedin* and aircraft from the carrier *Eagle*. The only consolation for Metzler was that he was not the only one in the pickle. *U103* (Viktor Schütze), *U107* (Günter Hessler) and the massive *UA* (Hans Eckermann) were stranded as well. They met to share a few spare parts and some lubricating oil, but no one had any fuel to spare. Returning home was going to be a problem and there was no way *U69* could reach France with what was still left in the bunkers.

It was shortly after lunch on 22 June 1941 when a welcome signal from headquarters was laid in front of Metzler. 'Refuelling established for 30 June at Culebra [the code-name for the supply ship *Charlotte Schliemann* in Las Palmas harbour in the Canary Islands]. Make an appointment three days before arrival. Do not take any more fuel than is necessary for your return journey to Lorient.'

Despite the problems the men had to put up with on a mission that had already lasted 52 days, *U69* kept running

into suitable targets and even, at this stage, attacked a convoy from which Metzler torpedoed three ships, although it looks as if only two were sunk. The U-boat Command urged him to continue shadowing the merchant ships until other boats could be drawn in, to which he politely replied that such a course of action had also been on his mind but was impossible due to the acute shortage of fuel, of which headquarters had already been informed. Such provocative instructions from home hardly helped smooth over an increasingly difficult atmosphere caused by a suspected attack of appendicitis aboard. Watching a colleague in agony batters deeply at morale, especially when one realises that he is likely to die because one cannot reach the elementary facilities which are taken for granted at home. Standing by totally helplessly is not easy, though this time the U-boat Command did help by telling Metzler to hand the patient over to the supply ship in Las Palmas.

Two days later, Metzler recorded in his diary that he was positioned off Las Palmas. Being so close to land without being allowed to step on it after such a long time at sea was indeed a bitter pill. But then, it was war and they were seamen who were expected to give their last, and no one complained more than the normal groans. In a way, Metzler was pleased when his men complained. He knew that things would be really bad if they stopped. Complaining was part of everyday life.

In the end, it was during the dead of night, at almost 02.00hrs on 30 June 1941 when U69 was made fast by the side of the *Charlotte Schliemann*. The whole operation had been so well prepared that the transfer went exceptionally smoothly. The sick seaman was transferred, fresh fruit, vegetables, meat and other goodies were passed over while the oil flowed and shortly before first light, at 05.30hrs, U69 was back at sea, heading home to Lorient.

The men who landed on the Canary Islands for an unscheduled holiday in April 1943 were from U167 under Korvkpt Kurt Sturm. He came to this boat because the first commander, Kptlt Kurt Neubert, had been seriously injured during a heavy storm while on his first operational war voyage. The first watch officer, Günter Zahnow, took over command to drive the boat to Lorient. New commander Sturm then guided U167 into calmer southern waters where it became part of a patrol line searching for a well-protected convoy. The air cover proved most determined and skilled. Coming under attack from two aircraft, one after the other, the men did not even have time to repair the damage from the first before they had to work even harder when the second added drastically to their life-threatening problems. Engines had been unseated, one of the shafts was bent, compressors no longer worked, batteries had cracked and there was a long list of other catastrophes. Sturm had no choice other than to contemplate abandoning ship. The only plus point was that sufficient life remained in the batteries to reach the nearby Canary Islands. A number of men were also in a bad way, while Günter Zahnow was seriously injured. Yet, Sturm was not the type to give up easily and he drove his men into a thorough damage evaluation before making his final decision to scuttle his boat. This showed that there was no way that he was going to get the boat back to France, making the option of scuttling near the Canary Islands by far the most attractive choice.

It was possible to take bearings on a number of lights so that U167 could creep safely close to a beach where men could swim ashore without being battered to death by waves hitting an array of sharp rocks. Not enough undamaged life-rafts remained, so only the injured could be accommodated in them. The bay at Las Burras on Gran Canaria was chosen for the landing because it was well away from the main centres, but had a good-sized fishing fleet which might help in bringing men ashore. Everything went relatively smoothly. Günter Seidel (engineering officer), Helmut Maerz (Obersteuermann), Hans-Joachim Fuchs (Dieselmaat) and Ernst Semmel (watch officer) remained on board with the commander once everybody else had left. The remaining power was going to be used to take the boat back out to sea into deeper water for scuttling. However, this did not run according to plan. U167 had not gone very far when Sturm shouted for the men down below to come up instantly. They had hardly reached the top of the conning tower when waves washed them off and the boat disappeared from under them. Obviously something had gone wrong, but at least no one lost his life.

In the meantime, local fishermen had been alerted and, in time-honoured tradition, launched their boats to help those in distress. A number of Germans were picked up and some who reached the beach on their own found themselves being helped ashore through the dangerous surf. Communications were good for such a quiet and out-of-the-way location and the following day a boat turned up to take the entire crew to Las Palmas. This transfer took place during the hours of darkness, to prevent eavesdroppers or awkward authorities from interfering. Everybody was quickly brought out of sight aboard the *Charlotte Schliemann*.

According to international rules, military personnel who land in a neutral country should be interned for the duration of a war. Civilians, including men from the merchant marine, were allowed to move about freely so the U-boat crew had to be disguised. One must marvel at the efficiency of those men responsible for running ships like *Charlotte Schliemann*. Being constantly scrutinised by all manner of hostile observers meant they had to work under cover and, despite all the problems, in this case they still managed to produce 53 sets of civilian gear in very short order. These arrived by lorry during the depths of night, two days after the men. In that short time a Spanish supplier had collected together everything each man might need, from a toothbrush to a variety of clothing. Even a case, for carrying the new possessions, was provided. The man who arranged all this and paid the supplier, the German consul Harald Flick, remained on the Canary Islands after the war to set up business as a main dealer for a well-known German car manufacturer. Maschinenmaat Hans-Joachim Fuchs from U167 was one who felt quite at home aboard the German supply ship. This was his second visit, having been once before while serving in U103 under Viktor Schütze.

To make the whole incident even more eventful, the men from U167 were not confined to the inside of the *Charlotte Schliemann* for long. After a detailed briefing, they were allowed ashore into a warm world the majority of them had not even dreamt about. Sufficient Germans, cut off by the war and pleased to see new faces, were available to guide them through a magical summer island holiday.

Sadly, the welcome break did not last long. The U-boat Command was determined to get the men back before the enemy interfered and prevented their return. In the dead of night, the men boarded a tug to be taken out to sea where they met U455 (Hans-Martin Scheibe). Even this difficult move was carried out with style. The men were transferred by breeches-buoy, hardly getting wet and without losing a single suitcase. They had landed virtually empty-handed from their wrecked boat, but acquired a good number of souvenirs during their enforced stay. Squashing back into a U-boat's exceptionally cramped quarters was a dramatic change of circumstances, but the majority quickly settled down. The passage home was soon also made more bearable by distributing some of their crew to a number of other U-boats. U154 (Oskar-Heinz Kusch) U159 (Helmut Witte) and U518 (Friedrich-Wilhelm Wissmann) helped to make the cramped situation more bearable.

Once back, the men enjoyed a brief home leave before the majority met again in the Baltic for the commissioning of U547. The commander, Korvkpt Kurt Sturm was flown home. Günter Seidel, the engineering officer, benefited most from the disaster by being detailed to remain behind to search the seas for any secrets which might float to the surface and also to keep an eye on the sinking site in case the opposition got wind of the position and started taking an interest in the wreck. He was fortunate enough to remain on the idyllic summer island for another 18 months before being brought back home.

Chapter 9
The Barren Arctic

Above: The acquisition of Arctic gear was not a great problem in the German navy because the extremely cold winters along the eastern Baltic assured the quartermaster's stores kept a good supply of suitable clothing.

One of the first boats to carry out landings in the Arctic was *U377* which entered into the myriad fjords around New Alesund during the autumn of 1942, first to set up a land-based automatic weather station similar to the one erected by *U537* in Canada and then to install a manned weather base on Cape Mitra. A number of these functioned successfully in the Arctic throughout the war, with bases in Greenland and the islands further to the east of Spitzbergen. The stories of many of these are still shrouded in mystery, awaiting keen historians to unravel what will probably be a fascinating chain of events. The men who manned these bases were a special breed who relished the loneliness of harsh isolation and were capable of looking after themselves in the inhospitable climate of the long Arctic night. But it was not entirely a realm for men. Shortly after the war a woman spent a winter with her husband and his friend in one of Spitzbergen's isolated huts. Christiane Ritter's fantastic book on this experience still provides one of the best insights into the harsh life in the darkness of the bitter north. During the war, her husband had over-wintered on Spitzbergen as a member of one of the German weather teams.

U212 LANDING ON BEAR ISLAND

U212 (Kptlt Helmut Vogler) was one of those little known boats which occupies a large space on the bronze wall plaques of the U-boat memorial because her entire complement of 49 men was killed when the boat was sunk by HMS *Curzon* (Lt A. Diggens) and HMS *Eskins* (Lt G. Bonner-Davis) in the English Channel to the south of Brighton on 21 July 1944. Commissioned towards the end of April 1942, the boat survived for a considerable period against heavy odds, putting out to sea on no less than 17 occasions, but in all that time had never sunk a single ship. That is not to say that her existence was without interest, for Vogler had attacked several targets and was at the receiving end of many depth charge detonations.

Above: One advantage of the Arctic seas as far north as Spitzbergen is that they are often ice-free for most of the year, making progress through them relatively easy going. However, coping with near freezing temperatures while soaked to the skin and standing on lookout duty for periods of up to four hours was not a comfortable undertaking.

Right: The duty watch of *U251* demonstrating the type of fashions worn in the cold Arctic. The outer garment is a special leather jacket with the fur side inwards to provide an additional layer of warmth on top of normal coats.

Above: Gun layers of *U212* preparing the 88mm for action. This weapon could be controlled from both sides and usually required one man to adjust the elevation and another to traverse it. Both could look simultaneously through the sight, which is seen attached to the side of the gun. Another man was usually required to load the weapon and an officer stood by to oversee the procedure. On top of this, when a larger number of shells were going to be shot, a chain of carriers was required to bring up the ammunition from a storage locker beneath the radio room.

His most embarrassing moment began early on 16 June 1943. A light northeasterly with heavy drizzle was sweeping over a calm but desolate Arctic sea when he signalled, 'From *U212* to BdU. Destroyer bearing 290°, brightly painted.' This was followed 20min later by, 'From *U212* to BdU. Destroyer on easterly course, normal speed, in grid square AB6364.' Imagine the red faces a few minutes later when another message went on air. 'From *U212* to BdU. Cancel previous signals. Destroyer is an iceberg.' Sadly, it was too dull to photograph the iceberg and show the startling similarity to a ship — it even seemed to have a bridge and a couple of funnels.

Grid square AB6364 lay some 800km north of the Arctic Circle, about half-way between northern Norway and Spitzbergen. The only feature in the area is Bear Island, usually a remote speck in the restless ocean, but in 1943 one frequently seen by Allied and German warships, protecting and attacking convoys running to and from North Russia. Sailors in those waters must have had, or they had to cultivate, a stout indifference to cold, wet weather. Even on dry days, without rain, there was always the chance of finding one's quarters damp from the spray thrown up by choppy waters and from condensation dripping or even streaming down cold metal walls. Despite these drawbacks, *U212* was having a relatively placid time. Eternal daylight, from the midnight sun, and relatively forgiving conditions meant life was just about as boring as it could get. Only the repetitive drudgery of daily chores kept the men on their toes.

It was shortly before the evening meal, a couple of days after the iceberg incident, when the radio operator handed the commander a signal. 'Assume that there is an enemy radio or meteorological station on the north coast of Bear Island at the mining settlement of Tunheim. This target was bombed by the Luftwaffe and there are no signs of life. As soon as the weather and your general situation permits, approach the settlement with extreme caution and land a reconnaissance group. Report on the condition of the station. Your absence from your present patrol area is to be as brief as possible. Report when you leave your operations area and when the mission has been completed.'

Helmut Vogler could hardly believe the order. He read and then re-read the signal before looking up and tossing it onto the table for others to examine. They had never done anything like this before. Assembling the reconnaissance party was not difficult, however. Everybody was keen on going ashore and Vogler decided that one officer should be landed with seven men. The next trick was to find out whether their small arms were in serviceable condition. Hardly ever used and stored in well-packed boxes, they were not handled very often. After this the men had to think about what they could carry. In the end, the landing party was to be equipped as follows:

- Officer and warrant officer: each to carry a machine pistol with four filled magazines, a pistol with 50 rounds of ammunition, a double-barrelled signal pistol with five red, five green and five white cartridges, binoculars and four hand grenades.

- Petty officer: a machine pistol with four filled magazines, a pistol with 50 rounds of ammunition, four demolition charges with time-delay detonators, four hand grenades and binoculars.

- Radio petty officer: a pistol with 50 rounds, four hand grenades, bag with special tools including a variety of screwdrivers and a hammer, all wrapped in a life-jacket.

- Two men: each with a pistol and 50 rounds, four hand grenades, 300 rounds of ammunition for the machine pistols. Matrosengefreiter and signalman Bittner also to take a set of signal flags and binoculars.

- Two men: each with a pistol and 50 rounds, four hand grenades, three throwing ropes for making fast the inflatable dinghy.

- Each man to wear a life-jacket.

Everything was checked and double-checked, a signalling plan devised and the details fully discussed while Vogler manoeuvred the boat towards the coast. After observing the target area through the periscope on and off for some time he came to the conclusion that there was likely to be no resistance, but the absence of a suitable landing stage meant the men were going to row ashore in a couple of inflatables. For this reason they were divided into a reconnaissance party and a security group, so that the transport should not get lost. Now, imagine the scene. Eight armed men with butterflies in their stomachs waiting by the central control room for the all-clear to clamber up onto the upper deck with their heavy equipment. Once outside, the large inflatables were brought out of their storage lockers. The handles of inflation canisters were pulled and then the air hissed out of holes pierced through the rubber during the earlier sharp weather. The intrepid landing party was ready, but had no means of getting ashore. Of course, such things never happen in films, but this was reality and the men had to think of something. Not to be put off, they brought up a good number of life-jackets as well as shoring timber for repairing leaks and all this was lashed together into a raft. Yes, this does rhyme with daft, but the idea worked and got IWO Friedrich Stege and Bootsmaat Ziegert ashore.

Tunheim, on the northeast side of Bear Island, had a pier with a narrow gauge railway running to a coal mine further up in the hills, behind a tiny group of huts and dormitories for the workers. It would have made an ideal landing place, but had been abandoned some time ago and looked rather rickety. It was also rather high for a low submarine to make fast to, with no safe-looking ladder for climbing up. In any case, it was an obvious place for a possible defender to aim his guns, so Vogler took the safer alternative and decided to unload the makeshift raft near a well-sheltered beach.

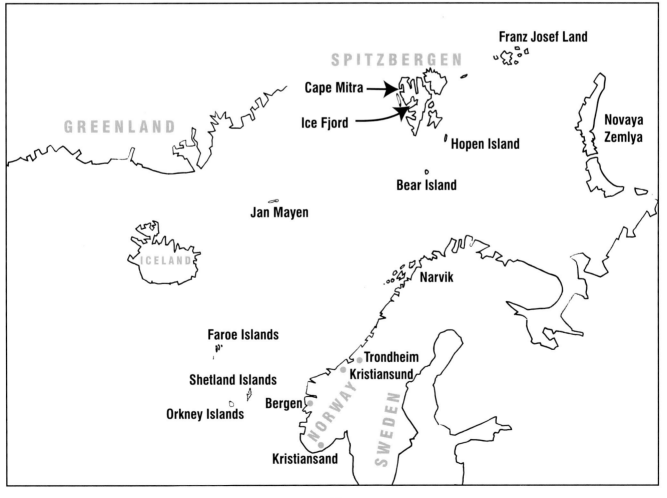

Above: U212 under Kptlt Helmut Vogler approaching Tunheim on the northeast coast of Bear Island. The three crosses mark the position of the old pier, while the cross in the sky indicates the radio mast, and the single cross in the water, the landing beach.

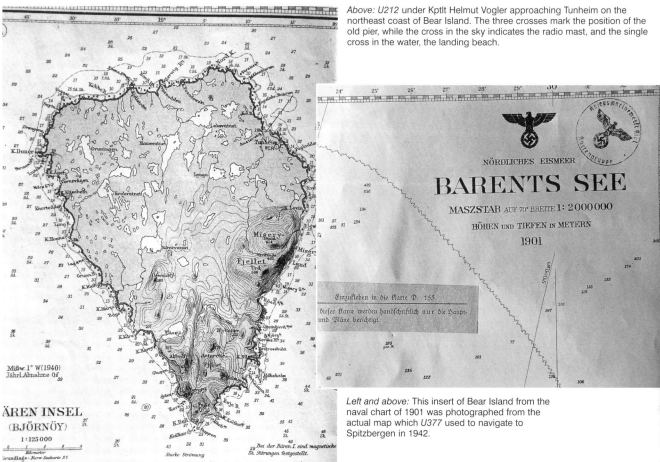

Left and above: This insert of Bear Island from the naval chart of 1901 was photographed from the actual map which *U377* used to navigate to Spitzbergen in 1942.

Left: U212 with conning tower still in pristine condition, shortly after having been commissioned. The white mark on the side, made up of two triangles, was an identification mark used during training in the Baltic. The emblem on the front of the tower is the coat of arms from the area of Bad Oldesloe (between Hamburg and Lübeck), home town of the commander, Helmut Vogler, which had adopted the boat and crew. The hump at the base of the tower contains the magnetic compass, which could be viewed by the helmsman down below through an illuminated periscope. The upper deck planking was about a metre above the pressure hull and the space below it was used to accommodate a number of items such as life-rafts.

Below: A water and pressure-resistant container lying on the rotting deck of *U534*, which is now being restored as a museum by the Warship Preservation Trust in Birkenhead (England). A number of these fitted vertically under the upper deck.

Then, moving in to about 150m from the shore, a shudder and a deep grating noise brought the submarine to an unexpected standstill, followed by a report from the bow torpedo compartment that one of the tubes had started leaking. Now, suddenly, there might be a demand for that shoring timber, but most of it was already under way. It took the two men the best part of 15min to paddle the clumsy contraption over that comparatively short distance while the engines pulled the boat clear of the obstruction. Luckily there appeared to be no major damage.

Bursting into the first building, the two-man landing party discovered a pile of dynamite and guessed that this was the explosive store for the mine. Most of the radio masts looked rather dilapidated, but one was rather substantial and, finding the place deserted, Stege decided to blow it up with dynamite from the first hut. This produced masses of smoke, a lot of noise and hurled debris through the air, but did very little damage to the iron structure. The second charge twisted it out of shape. Satisfied with their effort, the men turned their attention to the other buildings. The equipment in them had rusted considerably, meaning it was not necessary to demolish it any further. Radios and other items of interest were not discovered. The newspapers were old and the few items which looked useful were damaged beyond use. The earlier Luftwaffe bombs had done their job pretty well.

There was certainly no trace of a weather station. The men made a special, thorough search for it, but did not find anything incriminating. There were no signs of recent human habitation and eventually they plodded back down to the beach. There was one tense moment when an aircraft swept low over the island, but it was identified as a Blohm und Voss flying boat and quickly sent the correct German recognition signal, allowing everybody to breathe a sigh of relief. Soon the U-boat closed in on the beach once more to retrieve the landing party and shortly afterwards Vogler could send the signal indicating that the mission had been successfully accomplished and return to the usual mundane patrol duty. The excitement was not quite over, for, two hours later, another aircraft appeared, probably a Junkers 88, but Vogler did not hang about to identify its nationality. Instead U212 dropped into the cellar. There was no point eating breakfast in a precarious position, when U-boats had the advantage of resting in the calm peace provided by the depths.

U703 RESCUES RUSSIANS FROM HOPEN ISLAND

In works of fiction one is usually confronted with a lengthy preparation period leading up to the climax of the story. Yet, reality is often quite different. The time when U703 was sent on a reconnaissance to Hopen Island was just as haphazard as U202's visit to Bear Island. This unforeseen task fell to ObltzS Joachim Brünner of U703 also in June 1943.

Brünner was killed a year later together with the rest of his men, but the second watch officer, LtzS Heinz Schlott, had in the meantime been promoted to train as commander for one of the new Type XXI boats. After the war, he recorded some of the astonishing events which took place in the deepest Arctic. In naval records, Schlott's Christian name is given as Heinrich, but his articles have been published under the name of Heinz, so there is a discrepancy somewhere. The information in this chapter is based on Schlott's writings, as a participant in the events described. Therefore, it is assumed that articles which claim that the evacuation described at the end of the section was carried out by U354 are cases of mistaken identity, though U354 did later fetch a German weather team from Hopen Island.

By this time U703 had already seen bitter action, having been thrown against North Russian convoys in dreadful conditions. In July 1943 the boat was on patrol in the cold once more when a radio signal brought unexpected orders, 'From Admiral Polar Seas to U703. A hut with three men has been discovered on Hopen Island. Carry out a general reconnaissance. If they are part of enemy activity then destroy their base.' Such instructions sound simple enough, but Hopen Island is some 35 kilometres long and about 4 kilometres wide, so finding a hut among the rock-strewn desolation was not necessarily the easiest of tasks.

Locating the island was not too difficult to start with. The weather was reasonably clear and the dark 500-metre high mountains stood out from the shimmering sea. Yet, the run-in to the coast proved quite difficult. U703 was still well over 1km from these inhospitable rocks when the echo-sounder reported that there were only a few metres of water under the keel, making it obvious that going much closer could end in possible disaster.

Scouring the land with binoculars from that considerable distance quickly brought results. A hut was discovered. All weapons were ready for action so Brünner gave the order to approach closer. Not wanting to rely solely on the echo-sounder, he had a couple of men in the bows sounding the old-fashioned way with a lead line. Nothing stirred. So Brünner gave the order for a few shots to be fired over the top of the hut, hoping that anyone sleeping inside might be woken by the commotion. Nothing. Then a dinghy was made ready and Schlott and three seamen paddled ashore. The small beach they were making for was littered with timber and other flotsam, but landing was not too difficult, although somewhat wet for the feet. Making their way up to the hut, they found it empty. A 20-year-old newspaper, some rotting coffee beans and other junk, together with the valuable timber on the beach, suggested that the place had not been occupied for some time. This was certainly not the hut reported by the Luftwaffe.

With the landing party back on board, U703 continued its search, once more keeping a respectful distance from the rocky shore. Some time later, they came upon a larger hut. Gunfire over its roof produced the figure of a man, waving his arms. When the landing party reached him, he stood terrified, with his hands in the air. A conversation was hardly possible since no one could find a common language, but after a little experimenting Schlott guessed that he was Russian. Later, patience, warmth and food enabled him to work out that the bedraggled man was Captain Beliaev of the freighter Dekabrist, which had been sunk by a Ju-88 on 4 November 1942. The captain had survived against incredible odds for nine long months in the most inhospitable region of the world.

Captain Beliaev's ship was part of an Allied experiment to send lone freighters to North Russia, one after the other with a couple of days' gap between them. This plan had worked reasonably well, with loss rates slightly better than for convoys travelling around the same time. Unfortunately, the 7,563grt Dekabrist was one which did not make it. A closer inspection of the hut showed that Beliaev was fortunate that his ship went down very slowly, making it possible to load considerable supplies into the lifeboats — he still had sufficient for some time ahead. He handed Schlott his revolver and a rifle with ammunition and showed him the evidence that he had shot a number of polar bears. The skins of these were in such good condition that Schlott took one home to use as a rug. Using sign language, some English and plenty of loud noises, the captain announced that there were three more people in

Left: Men on the bridge of *U703* under ObltzS Joachim Brünner. In the background is Obersteuermann Willy Grönegres, who later served aboard *U1222*.

Right: Lookouts on *U703's* bridge while approaching the Arctic islands of Novaya Zemlya. The raised periscope can be seen in the middle. The circular aerial of a radar detector on the left indicates that this was taken during the second half of the war.

another hut further along the shore. What was more, one of them was a woman, a lady doctor.

Moving on, U703 used the same trick of shooting over the roof of the next hut. This time it produced three characters, one of them with a megaphone, who shouted something in Russian. Then, the three made their way down to the beach, boarded a small boat and rowed out to the U-boat. Despite their ragged and somewhat weathered appearance, they looked in reasonable condition, though the older man was obviously not well. They were hardly on board when a violent shudder almost threw them off their feet. U703 had made contact with Hopen Island and the mechanical division set about establishing the damage, while Schlott rowed over in the borrowed boat to examine the hut. There was still the chance that these people were not telling the truth and had been engaged in some military activity. However, no such evidence could be found and the condition of the hut matched their story.

Once back on the submarine, Brünner told Schlott that they would take the captain back to Norway but the other three would have to remain behind. Brünner's argument was that the additional people could jeopardise the operational efficiency of the boat. Trying to understand his reasoning today, more than 50 years after the event, is virtually impossible. Therefore, it would seem pointless to attempt any explanation of this apparently heartless resolution, other than to point out that it was war, where the lives and comfort of ordinary people had been ground into disregard. People were suffering all over Europe, with weekly death tolls rising well into the thousands. Although the two men and the woman were well provided for from U703's supplies, seeing them struggle back to their lonely island was not easy for the men in the submarine.

A couple of months later, U703 was once more on patrol in the Arctic. On 2 October 1943 an order came from the U-boat Command to return home, but much to everybody's joy there followed the instruction to bring the three people from Hopen Island as well. Getting them off the island, on this occasion through a precarious surf, was incredibly difficult, especially as the younger man had been lying seriously ill in the hut for some time and had come to terms with the fact that he would die in that barren wilderness. The Germans went to considerable lengths to bring him into the submarine, but sadly he died before they reached Norway. The other two became prisoners of war.

The men from U703 were not so lucky. Shortly afterwards they all went down with their boat.

We do not know now who those three people were, where they had come from, why they were travelling in a ship to Russia and what became of them afterwards. Had it not been for a brief encounter with U703, to have had a small part of their lives recorded in the boat's log and for Schlott to have elucidated these bare facts, those four would have vanished from this earth without having left any mark at all.

ARCTIC RECONNAISSANCE
Kptlt Günter La Baume left a stressful office job at the Supreme Naval Command a few days before his 30th birthday to endure the discomforts of initial submarine training. Five months later, towards the beginning of September 1941, he went through a commanders' course and at the same time learned about the technicalities of his first command. His boat, U355, was being built in Flensburg, not far from the naval officers' school where he had started his military education way back in 1929. Things had changed since La Baume's first visit as an 18-year-old cadet from Danzig. The old haunts around the harbour were still the same and the red brick 'castle' for the 'Lords of Mürwik' still dominated the scene, only now everything was adorned with swastikas and the town was on a definite war footing.

La Baume was lucky. His first voyage took him north into the polar seas, where he took part in the attack on Convoy PQ17 and even succeeded in sinking the 5082-ton freighter SS Hartlebury near the desolate islands of Novaya Zemlya. Such a baptism of fire lured many into a false sense of what to follow. Instead of an abundance of targets, La Baume found a different type of enemy. Remaining north of the Arctic Circle, he learned to cope with the elements always presenting the unexpected at a time when it was least required. Yet, the hard lessons of the polar seas contributed to the men remaining alive. A year later, La Baume was still commanding his old boat, but with a good number of new faces. Many of the men with whom he commissioned U355 had moved on to receive promotion and to die elsewhere.

Those who remained with U355 were lucky to have missed Black May in 1943, when over 40 U-boats were sunk. At that fateful time, U355 was lying in Trondheim (Norway) for considerable modification. A radar set was built in, the large 88mm deck gun was removed, the gun platform on the conning tower was enlarged and another one added lower down to hold a 37mm or quadruple 20mm anti-aircraft gun. This spell in dock provided the welcome opportunity to enjoy a brief period of home leave, something which U-boat men did not manage very often.

The U-boat had only just departed on its next patrol when the crew were startled by a sudden change of course. La Baume was not the type to keep his men in the dark and it was not long before the intercom crackled into life with the news that an aircraft carrier, three cruisers and nine destroyers had been sighted. Every U-boat in the area was being pulled into a tight patrol line. The fact that the boat was now going at full speed was not appreciated by the majority of the crew. They had already had to shoot several drifting mines and at top speed these possible obstacles would be even harder to avoid. The men guessed that the mines had been torn loose from their anchors in British waters and had drifted northeastwards to Norway on their own. The gloomy conversation was still centred around the mines, the high speed and the Royal Navy squadron when it became clear that the machinery was not terribly happy to obey the orders from the U-boat Command either.

The engine room staff had been running around for some time, not quite sure what had thrown so many gremlins into their realm. Coughing and choking engines were not very agreeable to live with, especially when the problem had never occurred before and when they had always behaved themselves in the past. A couple of days later the men discovered the culprit inside the fuel filters: bronze paint. The insides of the fuel bunkers had been painted during the recent overhaul but with the wrong type of paint. The fuel had washed it off and reduced it to a shimmering bronze sludge which collected in the thin fuel injection jets. Of course, once these were blocked there was no hope of the engines responding in the way they should. There was nothing for it. La Baume sent off one of those terse signals and then made for Norway to have the bunkers pumped out. The men were delighted by the diversion. There was always the hope of leave, but this time they did not get a great deal of peace nor the chance to step ashore. The authorities took advantage of the situation by stocking the boat up with provisions at the depot ship Kärnten, away from civilisation, and then U355 was on its way back out to sea.

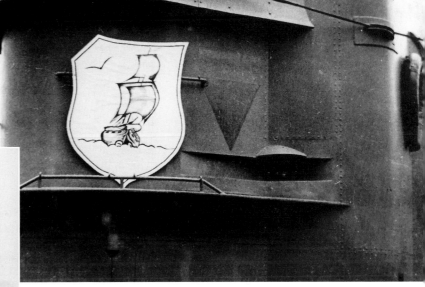

Above: U703 sailing through the Arctic in the summer of 1944.

Above: The conning tower of *U703*. This shows the emblem in its development stage. Later it was painted in full colour and with greater details, as well as a cross on the foremost sail. The lip on the conning tower seen at the bottom of the picture was often called the spray deflector, while the uppermost lip was known as the wind deflector. A lifebelt can be seen hanging on the conning tower wall towards the right.

Left: Two men from *U703* on one of the Russian islands of Novaya Zemlya

Left: Men from *U703* on the beach at Novaya Zemlya. They are wearing standard issue life-jackets over their clothing.

Below: *U703* exploring Hopen Island. The men were expecting a counter-attack from a possible Allied base on the island and therefore mounted a good number of light machine guns on the top of the conning tower. The vertical pole on the left is the partly raised rod aerial.

Bottom left: Obersteuermann Willy Grönegres of *U702* wearing special sunglasses. These were attached firmly to the face and were designed for the binoculars to be butted onto. This system was thought to have had an advantage over binoculars with in-built filters by not changing the light intensity when the lookout put them down.

Heading north, La Baume told his men that this time they were on their way to Spitzbergen for a general reconnaissance. Apparently the Luftwaffe had regularly reported a number of enemy ships in those waters, making the High Command think that there must be some form of Allied activity on the barren island. Before the war, it had been a domain of hunters, whalers and coal miners, but the last people to be stationed there had been forcibly evacuated by British and Canadian forces shortly after the beginning of the war. While this was in progress, soldiers also destroyed the mines, to prevent the coal from going towards the German war effort via Norway and, at the same time, set fire to the coal stocks waiting to be exported.

The first sight of Spitzbergen, in July 1943, could have been created from a picture book. High snow-covered mountains, ranging up as far as the low clouds, were half-hidden behind a white haze hanging low over the water. This low sea fog was promising. It enabled *U355* to approach unseen and the waters were not frozen, meaning they were unlikely to bump into ice. The plan had been to wait off shore until evening. Not so much to wait for darkness, because up in those latitudes the sun hardly sets during the summer, but people living on land were known to maintain a mid-European time-scale by sleeping during the 'night-time' hours. Therefore, La Baume wanted to take advantage of possibly meeting the opposition at a time when they were likely to be less attentive. Now, this fog offered the alternative of going in submerged, to get close to the major settlements for a quick examination through the periscope. The snag with underwater operations was that the crystal clear water would make it easy for a passing aircraft to spot the submerged submarine. However, the fog was preventing that from happening and by remaining under water, it was thought to be more likely to spot activity, such as smoke, rather than the calm when people were asleep.

It was around midday when La Baume took a stab at a submerged approach. Everybody was at action stations, as the boat headed towards the wide Ice Fjord. Progress was good. Everything seemed to go exceptionally well until La Baume raised the periscope inside the fjord and realised that although a few minutes earlier they had experienced a textbook example of sea fog, now there was none of it among the land-locked sheltered waters. Looking back, he could see the white curtain hanging in the distance, but in front and to both sides were crystal clear rocks rising high into the sky.

U355 surfaced and slowly crept towards Barentsburg, the largest settlement on Spitzbergen. There were no signs of life. The concrete pier and the houses were deserted. Only an eerie spiral of smoke drifted up from the coal dumps. These had by now been burning for a couple of years, smouldering slowly under a thick layer of ash. La Baume was not unduly perturbed. He knew about this phenomenon from *U377* (Kptlt Otto Köhler), which had discovered it almost a year earlier while calling in at New Alesund. Then, the men's attention was caught by what they took to be a man carrying a hurricane lamp. But, on closer examination, they found that the wind sometimes blew the ash away to allow very small flames to flicker up, almost as uncanny as the will-o'-the-wisp of the European marshlands. Slowly, *U355* moved along the coast while binoculars focused on every nook and cranny, but there were definitely no signs of life. A few huts left behind by hunters, the odd piece of wreckage, but nothing to suggest that the Allies were using the place for any military purpose.

At 16.36hrs there was suddenly a weird whistling noise followed by a splash in the water ahead of them. The men would usually have reacted much faster to such a characteristic sound, but somehow, up in that barren wilderness, no one imagined that it could be an artillery shell. The hollow booming detonation of the gun followed some time later, as a second shell hit the water. No one had spotted the gun and even after it had given away its presence, the men still could not determine its position. La Baume did not hang about for the gunners to get their range and the boat dropped into the depths, where several more shells were heard to hit the water. Whoever was up there, they appeared to be rather enthusiastic.

So far, the visit had been conducted in a leisurely, almost cruise ship, type of atmosphere. Now suddenly, hearts started beating again while La Baume examined the coast. The high magnification lens on the attack periscope was broken, so he stood in the central room, looking through the navigation periscope, but still he could not determine the location of the gun. There was some comment about the gun being of slightly larger calibre than the rifles used by seal hunters, but he did not make any effort to engage it. His orders were to carry out a reconnaissance, not to engage in a gun duel. Thankfully that could be left to others.

Twenty-four hours later, the gun had almost been forgotten, but the caution it had generated remained as *U355* approached a radio station in another fjord. It looked deserted, without any signs of life, except that the aerial mast stood defiantly among the conglomeration of dilapidated huts. Being about 30m high, it could be seen from a long way away. It did not look neglected enough, so La Baume ordered an armed landing party ashore. This prospect had been thoroughly discussed beforehand and the group could therefore be dispatched exceedingly quickly, but caution still ruled the roost. La Baume was not in a hurry and

Below: It is likely that the deck in the foreground is that of U1163 under ObltzS Ernst-Ludwig Balduhn. It appears to be exceedingly close to land. The boat installed a weather station on northern Norway and another one on Bear Island.

Left: Men from *U1163* ashore either in northern Norway or on Bear Island.

Right: Men from *U1163* rowing ashore either in northern Norway or on Bear Island.

Above: New Alesund on Spitzbergen, photographed before the tiny mining settlement was evacuated by Allied forces shortly after the beginning of the war. The main features for orientation are: (from left to right) the coal loading pier, the houses of New Alesund, the massive scaffold close to the sea towards the right is what remains of an airship hangar and the coal mine entrance can be seen towards the right.

Above: The pier at New Alesund, and a similar one on Bear Island, were designed for loading coal. Therefore they were high up so that tipper trucks could be rolled to the end and unloaded by dropping the contents into waiting ships. The height of these piers made them unsuitable for landings from U-boats.

Above: The railway running from the pier to the coal mine at New Alesund. Waste tips by the mine and the old airship hangar can be seen. Before the war both the Norwegians and the Italians based airships on Spitzbergen for a number of adventurous expeditions to the North Pole.

Left: Although the houses on Spitzbergen were quite substantial with good insulation, many of the isolated hunter's huts were built with whatever materials could be carried or were found washed up on the beaches. This is the radio hut of the weather station *Bassgeier* on Shannon Island during the summer of 1944.

Left: The warm current which carried a good quantity of timber to Spitzbergen and other Arctic islands also brought with it a more unwelcome cargo of mines, ripped from their original fields by storms. A large number of these were discovered in the Arctic seas by U-boats. These mines were designed to float with their spikes upwards, therefore being washed up on a beach did not necessarily detonate them. It is likely that this is a World War 1 mine discovered on the German North Sea coast before the war, but looks similar to the ones found by U-boats in the Arctic.

decided to wait for the early hours, when the inhabitants were more likely to be sleeping. It was 06.00hrs when four men paddled ashore, examined the huts, placed demolition charges on the mast and returned to the boat two hours later.

The expedition was into its eighth day when alarm bells erupted once more. Mast tips had been sighted. This was promising and offered the opportunity of making some room in the bow compartment by losing a few torpedoes. It was thought that this could well be a support vessel for the men who had shot at the boat and that it might be a good opportunity to get even with them. A ship on a northbound course had been reported by the Luftwaffe some time earlier. So things looked auspicious. The snag was that a look through the periscope suggested that the mast tips did not seem to move. Examining them again a few minutes later indicated that they were in exactly the same position as before. Surfacing again, the men laughed at themselves. They had spotted a couple of very thin rocks sticking up from the far-off shore. Yet, the tension had hardly subsided as the alarm shrilled once more. This time, a large aircraft was approaching. No one took the trouble to identify it. It could have been a German Condor or an Allied Liberator, but La Baume was not too keen on finding out.

The exploration of the polar fjords had become almost ordinary, with everybody on board having been given the opportunity to see some of the wonders of that natural world, when *U355* nosed into another of those deep rocky bays. The men were in the process of discussing the dangers of underwater rocks, when some 2km from land the boat touched bottom. Fortunately, La Baume was well prepared. The boat had been trimmed bow heavy and therefore it was simply a case of blowing the tanks to lift the bows a little higher and going astern to pull free. A noticeable jerk indicated that this had been successful and progress continued on one diesel engine, the other being used to recharge the batteries. Their course was suddenly somewhat erratic, however, with the boat wobbling about like a drunken sailor. Even a few orders to the helmsman for rapid changes in course did not rectify the problem. Something was wrong and, after considerable debate, it fell to the engineering officer, LtzS Rufer to go in for a swim. This had to be carefully planned. The water temperature was only four degrees above freezing, making it obvious that he could remain down for only a very brief period. Water was heated for a warm

drink and possible hot wash before he donned the emergency diving gear, fastened a rope around his waist and dropped off the stern. The men on deck watched the bubbles through the crystal clear water for hardly longer than a couple of minutes before he was back on deck, shivering and only just capable of saying that the propellers were in order but one of the two rudders was missing. Everybody breathed a sigh of relief. Being stranded up there in such hostile isolation without a means of getting home was not an encouraging prospect. The problem was solved by using the shaft with the functioning rudder when running on one engine and it was not serious enough to prevent the boat from returning home.

The boat was moving very slowly towards New Alesund, up in the desolate northwest, when another swimmer was spotted in the water ahead. This time, it turned out not to be human but another one of those dreaded mines. Finding them adrift so far north was not encouraging and a machine gun was brought up to sink it. The bigger anti-aircraft guns could not be used because they pointed over the stern and it would have been necessary to turn the boat round for them to shoot in the direction of the mine. At the tiny mining settlement, the men of *U355* found things in a similar condition to the way Kptlt Otto Köhler of *U377* had described them during the previous autumn. Convinced that there was no danger of an intrusion, La Baume allowed his men ashore, ostensibly for a brief reconnaissance, but also to pick up anything of use. The North Pole Hotel was just as *U377* had found it. The food on the tables had not yet gone rotten because it had been lying in deep freeze ever since the heating went off during the Allied evacuation way back in 1940. The bar was still well stocked. Everything had a haunted, ghostly feel to it.

In his final report Günter La Baume acknowledged that he and his men had been exceptionally lucky to enjoy the best of the Arctic weather. The winds had been moderate to good, the worst rain had been nothing more than a heavy, driving drizzle and there had been no snowstorms nor any difficult ice conditions. In addition to this, the radio had behaved itself better than in the Bear Island area. Reception had been brilliant, even while cruising among the high mountains.

La Baume had hardly handed that report in when he was told that his next mission was to help install a manned weather station on Spitzbergen.

Left: U355 under Kptlt Günter La Baume in northern Norway.

Below: The stern of *U534* at Birkenhead (England), showing just how vulnerable the delicate rudders were. Hanging down, they could easily be ripped off by a collision, which happened to *U355* while reconnoitring the coast of Spitzbergen.

Chapter 10
Arctic Meteorological Stations

U365 SAILS TO SPITZBERGEN

Although a good number of manned and unmanned weather stations were established throughout the Arctic, very few first-hand accounts have been left behind. Most of these events were hardly even recorded in logbooks. Often there is only the brief comment saying 'Special Mission Accomplished' to give any indication that something out of the ordinary took place. However, there are a few exceptions. Heimar Wedemeyer, the first commander of *U365*, has left a typescript in the U-Boot-Archiv giving his personal account of one such episode. This only survives because, in November 1944, a twist of fate promoted him to join the staff of the 14th U-Flotilla, just a few days before ObltzS Diether Todenhagen took *U365* on her last voyage from which no one returned.

Coincidentally, before his Arctic adventure, Wedemeyer had some experience of landing men on isolated shores, although the first time he participated in such an operation was in a considerably more friendly climate, along the fringes of the Sahara. Wedemeyer was first watch officer of *U66* during the events described in Chapter 6.

The involvement of *U365* shows how little consideration these difficult undertakings were given by the U-boat Command, where such operations were considered to be nothing more than side-shows when compared to the all-out battles of the convoy war. *U365* had been in dock for some time. An accident with a German minesweeper had torn open some diving tanks and damaged the propellers. Coming back from trials, *U365* ran into a massive flock of ducks. Wedemeyer cursed that they did not have a shotgun, handed the con over to the first watch officer, LtzS Günter Heinrich, and had a rifle brought up from below. He even scored a lucky hit on one of the birds. Seeing it drop onto the water, Heinrich ordered the deck to be trimmed under the surface, manoeuvred under the duck and then raised slowly while someone raced down to pick up the dinner before it was washed overboard again. There was not very much left of the bird, but the boat was shortly due to make fast to a pier belonging to a Luftwaffe seaplane squadron at Tromsö, so at least there would be something of interest on the menu when they invited the commanding officer to dinner.

On 12 October 1944 *U365* left the pier at Tromsö. It had been fitted out for another normal voyage into the hunting grounds of the Arctic seas, which meant it was crammed full of torpedoes and provisions. Only the commander knew that they were to undertake a special mission to install a two-man weather detachment on Spitzbergen. The practical issue of the undertaking really hit home when he saw masses of special stores on the pier, waiting to be loaded into the already full U-boat. First, Wedemeyer told his men about the forthcoming mission and then he left them with the headache of solving the problem of where to put the stores. At times, there were advantages to being in charge. One could leave the cursing and deal with important social matters, such as building good relations with one's hosts.

The two-man over-wintering team required considerably more equipment than the usual baggage allowance. They had to take food for two years (in case they were not picked up), their hut, scientific apparatus, oil for running generators, coal for heating, guns for hunting, clothing, emergency escape apparatus and more — the list is almost endless. Everything they were likely to need for a minimum of six winter months in the dark, cold Arctic night had to be taken along. In a few weeks' time the seas would freeze over, making any form of relief impossible. Fitting all this into the already cramped quarters of a submarine was incredibly difficult and by the time the task was complete, there was no room to walk around the gear. It was a case of crawling through the boat. Only the central control room remained reasonably clear because it was essential to get at the various levers, valves and instruments.

Above: It would be tempting to add the explanation 'U-boat in Arctic Seas' to this picture, but a closer examination shows that this is a Type IID. A caption on the original suggests it is probably *U137* under ObltzS Hans-Joachim Dierks. The presence of a U-boat in the background would suggest that this was taken in the Baltic. However, something is wrong because Dierks took command of *U137* in March 1945, two months before the end of the war, and that makes it rather late in the year for such severe weather conditions, even in the far eastern Baltic. Whatever, the picture gives a good impression of what U-boats frequently looked like while operating in the cold north.

Right: This clearly shows how difficult it was to keep weapons ready for an engagement in the cold Arctic.

Bottom: U600 (Kptlt Bernhard Zurmühlen), a Type VIIC, under harsh winter conditions. The boat spent most of its operational time in the Atlantic and hardly ventured into the Arctic seas, where conditions were even worse than those shown in these photographs. The sky or navigation periscope with large head lens is partly raised.

The officers' mess and even the commander's 'cabin' were filled with stacks of boxes and lengths of timber; even the emergency controls under the deck of the bow and stern compartments were inaccessible.

Then, when they thought the task was complete, another lorry arrived to pile more loads on the pier. Some of the more rugged equipment, boxes with coal and the rubber dinghies were accommodated on the outside, in the space between the pressure hull and the upper deck. The first signs of trouble appeared while this was going on. The inflatables had not been packed well enough. The jolting over rough roads had resulted in the rubber of one having been rubbed through to produce several holes. These were too large for repairing with the usual patches, meaning there was no alternative other than to discard the boat. Finding a replacement at such short notice was not possible and the men had to do without.

It was the afternoon of Thursday 12 October 1944 by the time everything was stacked. Wedemeyer was intent on departing before midnight because there was no way a unit of the German navy ever put to sea on a Friday if it was possible to avoid it, and U365 was not going to break this long-standing tradition and risk a spell of bad luck. As it so happened this was not so much of a problem. The last night rave-up had to be cancelled. The seaplanes had been through a serious battle. Several failed to come back and those that did had casualties aboard, meaning U365 cast off in a rather sombre atmosphere.

The perilous journey out into the open sea went without incident. An escort showed the way and there were no surprises lurking among the fjords. Controlling the heavily laden boat was not easy, but eventually a good trim was achieved and U365 nosed northwards in exceptional discomfort. The two weather men and their trainer from the army could hardly stretch their legs, yet they were cheerful and quickly integrated as honorary members of the crew. They were lucky that the typical summer fogs had gone and the boat slid over calm seas with only moderate to light winds during the long hours of darkness.

The further north the boat progressed, the more untypical the weather became and slowly the dense summer fogs returned, posing the rather pertinent question of how the men were supposed to find Spitzbergen without bumping into it first. The problem was solved by nature. Slowly, huge mountains seemed to lift out of nowhere to appear as black sheets, high over the swirling whiteness. Having spotted Spitzbergen, the next trick was to find a sheltered bay where the boat could be hidden among the clutter of ice and rocks. At the same time, Wedemeyer wanted to get as close in as possible to cut down the number of journeys with the inflatables needed to get everything ashore. He wrote that the mountains appeared to grow around them until the boat was dwarfed by overpowering rocks. Then, within 150m or so of the land, the anchor chain rattled out of its locker.

Surveying the scene, Wedemeyer was surprised by the surf. The surface of the water was smooth, with hardly a ripple, yet close to the land it suddenly frothed into noisy waves, reminding him of the time aboard U66 when he watched two of the crew being pinned on the beach by a sudden heavy swell. This time he had sufficient rope to span the gap between boat and land, so that the dinghies could be pulled back and forth safely with the minimum of effort. Manoeuvring a rubber dinghy is difficult at the best of times and virtually impossible once the wind and currents want to take it in a different direction. Although no one had been terribly active for some time, everybody was by now somewhat tired and Wedemeyer

decided that a good meal followed by a night's sleep was going to be the first order for the rest of the day.

The following morning, three men paddled one of the inflatables ashore to locate the best landing spot. Watched by lookouts in the conning tower and a small Arctic fox on the shore, the rest of the crew started preparing the other inflatables. They had brought a small outboard motor, but this was more trouble than it was worth and it quickly became evident that such inventions were still too much in their infancy to be of any practical use. Wedemeyer felt like throwing it overboard, but naval property was holy and therefore it had to be returned to the quartermaster back home, even if it did not work.

This time it was not the Atlantic swell with overpowering surf which was the problem, as it had been with U66, but the tide. The wind got up and the tidal stream washed so fast out of the fjord that it threatened to jeopardise the whole undertaking. It might have been better to move further inland, but Wedemeyer had discarded that idea when he noticed a massive glacier further along the coast. Thinking that ice breaking off the end could create difficult waves and possibly force the boat onto underlying rocks, he had gone for the option of remaining further out. The narrows where they were anchored were thought to be advantageous because the surrounding rocks offered some camouflage in case enemy aircraft appeared overhead. Everybody knew that they were sitting ducks if they came under attack.

The highly strenuous work progressed undisturbed, despite numerous problems for which the men were not properly equipped. On the beach, for example, they stood up to their knees in the ice cold water every time a dinghy needed unloading. Waterproof walking boots would have been most useful, but the men had to make do with the standard gear worn on the top of the conning tower in rough weather. This was ideal for standing still in, but rather clumsy when it came to moving about with heavy burdens, and some of the boxes were terribly heavy. Despite the cold, men sweated profusely, making the harsh wind an irritating obstacle in the proceedings. On top of this, the ropes became wet and it was not long before the majority of men had either been bathed in their own sweat or by the wetness around them.

The unpleasant work continued all day and throughout the following night, as tons of stores were moved along this most precarious route. Eventually, when the boat was empty, Wedemeyer decided to leave some of his men ashore to help with the erection of the hut and to get the radio up and running. Moving out into deeper water and then submerging, the rest of the crew set about tidying up the interior to get the boat back into battle order. Everything worked well, and the periscope popped up at the appointed time to observe the recognition signal from land. Nosing back towards the shore, Wedemeyer picked up his men and the lieutenant from the army who had trained the two meteorologists, waved at the weathermen for the last time and then turned to make for the open seas.

The weather station functioned very well. It remained there until the summer of 1945, several months after the end of the war, when the men were picked up again to be brought back to Norway.

U354 ON HOPEN ISLAND

Roughly 12 months before U365 installed the weather station on Spitzbergen, U354 (Kptlt Karl-Heinz Herbschleb) landed a weather team on Hopen Island, but this operation went far less smoothly. At 06.00hrs on 27 October 1943, one week after Herbschleb's 33rd birthday, his lookouts spotted the first signs

The fjords and coast of Spitzbergen photographed from U-boats during World War 2.

of land rising above a shimmering sea mist. The Hopen Island area had been plagued by bad visibility during the previous voyages and the men of *U354* had become used to it. Approaching so close to uncharted rocks in conditions like these was not a terribly calming exercise. Such a cold wind had been whistling over the conning tower that even the salt spray had frozen, making everybody's lives even more hazardous. The problem was that the ice penetrated into vents, preventing them from being shut for diving. The sea itself was slightly warmer so the only solution was to dive and wait for the ice to melt, hoping that the ballast pump was capable of expelling any intruding water in the meantime. This was not too difficult on this occasion and the boat submerged without problems for just long enough to clear the superstructure of any slippery surfaces which had collected during the previous few hours.

Surfacing again, ammunition was brought up and the guns were manned while Herbschleb slowly approached the land. He had plenty of experience of the Arctic, having fallen foul of unreliable charts with islands in the wrong places and false water depths, and he was not taking any risks. With the echosounder in action and men standing by with the lead line to ascertain correct depths, he closed in until the shallowness would allow him no further. He was making for a solitary hut, well hidden among some rocks on the top of steep cliffs. It would make an ideal base for the weather team, but first Herbschleb had to establish whether it was vacant. The 88mm deck gun hurled a shell close over the roof. The detonation produced no response, so the men reckoned that there was no one around to protest.

Anchoring first, a rubber dinghy was brought up from its storage container, but was found to have been worn through in several places. Dinghy number two did not fare much better. It managed a couple of journeys, but the flexible rubber bottom was too weak for the heavy cargo and quickly tore away in places. The dinghy did not sink, but did fill up with water so it could only be used to transport goods which did not mind getting wet. By this time, though, the men had discovered that the deserted hut also had its own transport in the form of a good-sized lifeboat. Unfortunately, it had not been used for some time and had seen better days. Yet, mending a few holes was not beyond their skills and it was soon pressed into service. Sadly, neither the tools nor the materials for mending leaks were substantial enough to cope with the rigours of the Arctic and the process had to become an ongoing venture. The main snag was that the wood around the edge of the holes was not much better than the holes themselves, meaning that there was not much to attach the repairs to. Yet, the cutter did manage a number of vital journeys with half loads and the third inflatable helped as well.

The cold wind continued blowing with enough force to freeze the surface of the sea, making the whole process even more difficult. Men were no longer paddling over waves, but battling against a hard, crunching barrier. The ice remained relatively thin, but threatened to rip the rubber inflatable to shreds. A year earlier, *U377* (Kptlt Otto Köhler) had overcome such problems by going to sleep for the night and waiting for the water to freeze over so that the men could walk over the ice and unload their cargo with sledges. The snag on this occasion was that no one knew what the weather was planning on doing and it very much looked as if it was only going to be irritating without any intention of locking the U-boat into anything substantial. The midnight weather forecast was not promising at all. It suggested things were going to get worse. At about the same time, a Morse lamp from the shore passed on the news

that the surf was no longer passable without risking the dinghies being overturned. Herbschleb cursed, asking in his log why the U-boat Arm could not supply suitable boats for unloading. He made the point that rigid, metal-hulled craft would have been much better than the flimsy rubber boats.

Cursing did not help. Neither did the U-boat Command, which sent a signal saying that Herbschleb was to hurry up. This signal had just been laid before the commander when one of the lookouts reported that the cutter had sunk near the beach with its entire load. Peering through his binoculars, Herbschleb could see men in the freezing water, struggling with a number of waterproof packages, guiding them towards the beach. He breathed a sigh of relief as he counted packages and men safely on land. Those who had gone ashore to make the hut habitable for the coming winter looked like filthy skivvies on a building site, but that could not be helped. The cutter was pulled out of the water, repaired once more and press-ganged back into service.

Herbschleb cursed again when the duty officer reported that the submarine was dragging its anchor. There was nothing for it other than to move around and find better ground, although that meant moving even further out in the bay. At least no one was inconvenienced by the move. The surf had got worse again, making it impossible for the small boats to get through, so the transfer of the cargo had come to another halt. Yet, despite the problems, the men eventually got the job done. Shortly after lunch on 31 October 1943, everybody cheered as the lookouts reported that Hopen Island was out of sight.

Below: The side of a conning tower and stern of a U-boat in cold seas.

Below: Arctic lookout.

Chapter 11
U722 Supplies the Garrison at St Nazaire

In the summer of 1944, after the D-Day invasion of Normandy, the Allied armies swept across France, cutting off, but not capturing, the German U-boat bases along the Atlantic coast. There was no point in risking unnecessary lives by attacking those strongholds since shutting down the overland supply routes rendered them virtually useless. Attempts to continue operating out of the French bases quickly faltered due to a lack of supplies, giving U-boats little alternative other than to launch their raids from Norway. Having made this move, it quickly became apparent that this was no temporary withdrawal. The deteriorating situation in France made it clear that there was no hope of ever returning to the Biscay ports. Not only was the Allied barrier at sea becoming increasingly effective, but their advancing armies were pushing some of the beaten remnants of the German land forces into the submarine bases from the landward side. Consequently, large numbers of German troops found themselves in ever-worsening siege conditions, where a general shortage of everything prevailed.

Strangely enough, this scarcity did not apply to every field and a good number of valuable items, such as radar sets and schnorkels, remained in French stores. Some of this material, together with a core of specialists, was loaded into U-boats and moved out under such incredibly dangerous conditions that most boats never reached their destination. One boat, *U256*, was sunk, raised again, and then cannibalised for spare parts before Heinrich Lehmann-Willenbrock took the wreck north. After reading an account of this effort in the first edition of my book *U-boats under the Swastika*, he remarked that it was not as bad as I had made out, saying that *U256* was still partially working and it did reach its destination. Although his men were volunteers, many of them did not share his recollection, saying it was a hellish ride with no one thinking that they would ever see land again.

Missions in the other direction, that is from Norway to France, became more important towards the end of the war as several boats were made ready to supply the besieged French garrisons. One boat which undertook such a mission was *U722* under ObltzS Hans-Heinrich Reimers, who had commissioned it in December 1943. Later, when the men had completed their training, they joined the 5th U-Flotilla in Kiel for final kitting out. It was one of those calm September days of 1944. Kiel was enjoying an Indian summer, giving the false impression that the war was miles away. The pull from the local bars and their willing girls was powerful and highly exhausting, meaning it was usually the early hours of the morning before the men collapsed into their beds. One night they had hardly dropped off to sleep when air raid sirens howled their unwelcome announcement of an imminent raid. Racing down to the harbour, the men found the diesels already running and the boat casting off without waiting for a head count. Quickly, *U722* surged out into the wide waters beyond the breakwater.

The air raid warning system was obviously most efficient. *U722* had almost reached the naval memorial at Laboe before the first explosions erupted and everybody realised this was not a false alarm. Continuing to drive his boat at reckless speed, Reimers watched tons of bombs fall close to the spot he had just vacated. At the same time anti-aircraft fire and a multitude of searchlights sweeping through the sky added a brilliant backdrop to the occasion. One incendiary actually fell onto *U722*, indicating that the aircraft were not terribly good at aiming. Anything hitting a U-boat so far out was way off target and could only benefit the people of Kiel. Incendiaries hardly troubled a submarine. Someone jumped down to kick the thing into the water before any significant damage could be done.

U722 had hardly reached the open sea when the thunderous booming subsided into uncanny silence, leaving only a good number of fires lighting up the dark sky as poignant leftovers of the raid. The following morning looked the same as all previous days, only this time the order 'Get ready to for sea' was for real. One lorry after another appeared with boxes and packages, all of which had to be stowed inside the cramped interior. Although searching for clues, the men could not find any indications of where they might be going, not until a number of boxes with the warning 'Land mines — High explosive' suggested a land destination not a sea mission. The fact that these were then stowed inside the torpedo tubes confirmed that the boat was definitely not going to tackle convoys.

Eventually, without fuss and without any great ceremony, *U722* cast off and nosed out into the Baltic in the direction of Norway. There appeared to be no great urgency to go anywhere. Instead of making for open water, Reimers headed into the shelter of the fjords to practise schnorkelling. Not once, but over and over again until it could be performed without thinking. Even when this had been accomplished, there were no signs of putting out to sea. Instead *U722* headed further north towards Bergen.

The serenity of the astounding mountainous landscape was shattered only once by an aircraft dropping out of a brilliant sun. The gunners were ready and the 37mm anti-aircraft fire kept the intruder at a distance. Everybody breathed a sigh of relief. There was rather a lot of high explosive on board to make such an intrusion most unwelcome.

U722 then refuelled in Bergen. Men were allowed ashore, although none of them had yet discovered their destination. It was only some time later, when the boat had settled down in the depths of the Atlantic, that Reimers announced that they were going to supply the garrison of 30,000 men in St Nazaire. Instantly, the men made the connection with the land mines and the sealed sacks of what felt like paper. They were carrying mail to keep up the morale of the stranded men.

Everybody on board knew about the situation in France and could guess that the passage to the Biscay ports was going to be a hard nut to crack. The plan was not to surface at all but to proceed on the silent electric motors at about 2–4kt during the day. Each night the schnorkel was going to be extended for a few hours to re-charge batteries, but submerged progress with the diesel engines was not going to be much faster. The biggest drawback was that the boat's basic design dated back to shortly after World War 1, when submarines hardly ever dived for more than the hours of daylight and usually only went down for very short periods to avoid the enemy. They did not have facilities for remaining down for any prolonged period. This meant that the men had to put up with more than the usual discomforts.

The head (lavatory), for example, was out of use during the day because the boat was too deep to pump out the contents, meaning long queues of almost 50 men appeared at night to make use of the single facility. Those who could not wait used buckets and had to store the smelly contents until night-time permitted them to be flushed away. Food started rotting, men were seasick, adding an indescribable stench to the usual disgusting smell of oil, exhaust fumes, sweat and eau-de-cologne. Yet, there were also a few plus points. The cook was a volunteer who had served an apprenticeship in a hotel and had the rare ability to conjure up tasty meals. Many men had not seen such interesting food for some time. It was certainly much better than the general standard served up in the land-based canteens.

The biggest obstacle was provided by the weather. Schnorkelling had gone quite well in the calm Norwegian fjords, but now a lively sea assured that waves often washed over the top of the headvalve, meaning the air pressure inside the boat was suddenly sharply reduced. This was more than just uncomfortable. Every time the headvalve closed, it was agony for the men. It was something they had not been trained for, nor even told about, and they were not too happy to put up with it for any length of time. Yet, there was nothing anyone could do. Everybody was pleased when the batteries were full and the damned mast could be lowered again. Ears were not made for such sudden variations in air pressure.

The dreadful thought after the first night was that this torture would have to be experienced every night for a hell of a long time. Those who looked at the chart in the central control room realised they were in for more than a quick visit to hell. The pencil line so far extended only as far as the Shetland Islands. The only consolation was the hope that the southern waters might be calmer, but it was already halfway through October 1944 and winter storms were likely to rule the roost. The prospects were not good. What was more, far-off depth charge detonations indicated that the boat was approaching a heavily defended area.

The cargo inside the boat was lying about a metre deep or so all over the floor, making it impossible to walk from one end to the other without having to bend double. To make matters even more difficult, there was nowhere for the men to stretch out. Even at meal times they sat hunched up on top of the tables, adding an almost unbearable dimension to the suffering provided by the dreadful schnorkelling discomforts. It was only the thought of so many men cut off without any news from home which kept them going. At the backs of their minds they knew that they might be offering those stranded in St Nazaire a slightly better Christmas, perhaps with some good news from home.

The constant high activity experienced during training gave way to a totally different regime, where boredom became the order of the day. Most of the crew were confined to a tiny area where they always saw the same faces, meaning conversation gradually came to such a halt that even jokes were not appreciated anymore. The tales of exciting runs ashore and the exchange of news about noteworthy bars no longer made any impact. Even reading was painful. Most lamps were switched off to conserve power and trying to focus on small print in the dim light was virtually impossible. Some tried playing cards, but even that had its limits. The trouble was that there was virtually nothing to do: hardly any duties for the majority of men; no lookouts on the conning tower; no distractions during the long boring days. Only the schnorkelling brought the men to their toes with indescribable discomforts and pain.

One day towards the west of Ireland, while preparing for another schnorkel run, the men noticed that it was exceptionally rough. Still well below periscope depth, the rocking indicated that the next few hours were going to be difficult. When the commander peered through the periscope, he unexpectedly ordered, 'Prepare to surface.' Men who had hardly moved for days on end raced to their posts. Trying to get into the rain gear without being able to stand up was a torture in itself, but quickly the boat rocked into the ferociousness of an Atlantic gale, something the men had not even been aware of in the deep depths. Water poured down the hatch as breakers washed over the conning tower, but Reimers ordered rubbish to be brought up for discarding. Bucket after bucket was tossed overboard to make the foul smelling interior more bearable. Reimers had not surfaced just for the men's comfort, but mainly to take advantage of a brilliantly clear night. He wanted to shoot the stars, to get an accurate fix to calculate the boats exact position. So far they had been navigating on dead reckoning and that sort of calculation was not good enough for finding such a small target as a harbour entrance.

Reimers had orders not to make contact with the enemy and to remain undetected at all costs. So, once the storm had provided the protection to take those sextant readings, he ordered the boat down to continue charging the batteries with the aid of the schnorkel. This time something even more unexpected than the usual discomforts nearly killed the men. The headvalve seemed to have jammed shut, causing the pressure inside to drop lower and lower until the diesel engines cut out. Noses were bleeding, ears were aching, heads were spinning, men were going through the most unbelievable contortions to throw off the pain. Orders were shouted, but men could not hear. It was strange to see people talking, but not to detect any sound other than an odious ringing in the head. All usual sounds seemed to have disappeared. Slowly, as the men recovered from the agony, they found it was not the headvalve at fault, but a human error. The air supply valve had been shut off by accident and very nearly killed the crew. This emphasised how alert everybody had to remain, making it necessary not only to do one's own job but also to watch that colleagues were doing theirs.

Luckily for U722, the weather improved the further south they travelled and the vicious reputation of the Bay of Biscay was nowhere to be seen. Instead of frustrating gales, the men were faced with calm seas. This made schnorkelling easier, but tended to increase the risk of detection by the Royal Air Force. The only consolation was that the traffic in and out of the French bases had virtually ceased. So, hopefully, the British had diverted a good proportion of their aircraft into hunting U-boats elsewhere or flying on bombing missions over the Reich.

To make matters even more precarious, Reimers decided the boat had to surface once more to ascertain the exact position. There was no point in stumbling upon the French coast without knowing exactly where they were. There were a good number of German minefields and they had to count on there

This page and overleaf: The 37mm twin anti-aircraft gun of *U534*. This weapon was exceedingly rare, having been fitted to only very few boats towards the end of the war. It proved to be considerably superior to the earlier single-barrelled version, but still did not have enough punch to prevent attacks by large, fast flying armoured aircraft.

being more Allied mines in the obvious harbour approaches, making it important to steer well away from both. The prospects of so much possible opposition regenerated considerable discussion, making the time pass quicker, but also led to irritability and cursing at whatever decisions were taken.

Despite the presence of many surface craft, the main threat to life was created by the crew; once again the men almost killed themselves. This happened during one of those unbelievably calm nights, when it was very difficult to realise that the boat was running just below the surface. The schnorkel was being raised, but the man waiting to open the exhaust valve turned the wheel before the diesels were started. This meant that there was no pressure inside the exhaust pipe to blow the water out, causing it to cascade down into the engine, filling several cylinders. Luckily, it only penetrated into one of the engines, leaving the other one in running order, but it did mean a much longer battery charging period and a considerable effort before the problem was rectified.

In the past U-boats had announced their arrival when close to land, to be met by minesweepers for the final run into harbour. This time things were going to be more difficult. No one could count on an escort and, on top of this, the men in *U722* had to hope that German gunners were not going to start shooting at them. Reimers tried using the echo-sounder to help his navigation, but every time he planned on switching it on, the operator on the sound detector heard such an

abundance of other noises that it was not wise to keep this loud advert running for any length of time. Progress was indeed most precarious.

The news that the French coast had been sighted through the periscope was greeted with loud cheers. It was so close that St Nazaire could be reached within a couple of hours on the surface, but Reimers did not dare go up top anymore. Instead he continued crawling along at two knots, making hardly any headway against the current. Then the echo-sounder reported only 50m of water below the keel, meaning that things could become somewhat tricky if the boat was discovered. The waters were clear enough for aircraft to spot the submerged submarine at periscope depth and therefore there was nothing for it other than to lie on the seabed and await darkness.

It was hardly dark when the boat's loudspeaker ordered everybody to action stations. Things were not easy. Delicate control was now called for to raise the boat without allowing it to break through the surface. Following this, the engineering officer carefully adjusted the trim before allowing the propellers to ease it slowly towards its destination. Everything was quiet. There appeared to be no enemy activity and the weather was being most co-operative. Yet, it was a lengthy undertaking and the news quickly spread that it would be dawn before they covered the relatively short distance to the shore and could run into port. The silence in the boat was almost more disturbing than the noises of danger. Everybody was on tenterhooks, wondering whether they would have the opportunity of going ashore or whether they would be wiped out during these last vulnerable minutes, like so many boats before.

Shortly before dawn, Reimers ordered the boat to periscope depth and exclaimed in amazement. Navigation could not have been better. *U722* was lying right in front of the harbour approaches. There was still a good possibility of being attacked by aircraft and, despite being so near, Reimers still did not take the risk of surfacing. Creeping closer into a brilliantly rising sun, the men waited tensely for the order to surface. Diesels sprang into life and shortly afterwards the order was given to assemble on the upper deck. Clambering up, the men were struck by the intensity of the sun, something most had not seen for the five weeks for which they had been confined to a tiny dark space where they could hardly move. Now, unexpectedly, they found a wave of relief flooding through their deprived bodies as the boat nosed into the massive submarine bunker. The men were thankful for a well-earned rest and I am grateful to Rudi Waiser for having recorded the events of this momentous voyage for the U-Boot-Archiv.

U722 was lucky that time. It left St Nazaire again on 7 December 1944, loaded with a variety of metals, to arrive in Bergen for the new year. However, the good fortune did not last. The boat was lost with all hands on 27 February 1945 close to the Island of Lewis in the Hebrides as a result of an attack by HMS *Fitzroy* (Lt-Cdr A. J. Miller), HMS *Redmill* (Lt G. Pitt) and HMS *Byron* (Lt J. B. Burfield).

Chapter 12
The Final Defiance

In 1945, as the Allied forces were drawing close to German bases, the navy made preparations to destroy its weapons and to scuttle the remains of the fleet. However, the terms of surrender demanded that everything should be handed over intact. This was very much against Grand Admiral Dönitz's wishes, but feeling there was no sensible alternative, he agreed and ordered that Operation *Regenbogen* ('Rainbow') should not be executed. Exactly what happened during those turbulent times is still a little unclear, but somehow commanders took it upon themselves to carry out a last act of defiance by sinking their own boats before the invading forces could claim them as prizes. Many saw no reason for co-operation, taking the view that the bloody slaughter could have been stopped a good time earlier, had the arrogant Allies not insisted on an unconditional surrender.

When called to task for his actions and asked who gave the order to scuttle, Ajax Bleichrodt (senior officer for U-boats in Wilhelmshaven) told the British admiral that he did not need orders to prevent the enemy from boarding his ships. When an aggressive interrogator almost screamed at him that the boats in his charge should have been handed over intact, he calmly replied that he would comply with that condition as soon as the boats at sea came home, but those lying on the seabed were sunk before the terms of surrender came into effect.

At first glance, Operation *Regenbogen* appeared to be a simple matter of scuttling submarines, but on closer examination it seems to have been quite a complicated procedure, with many U-boats making landings in difficult circumstances on shallow, isolated beaches. Stores were brought ashore, the welfare of the men was seen to and discipline maintained to prevent possible mutinies adding to the complications of the bitter defeat.

Above: U3503, a Type XXI under the command of ObltzS Hugo Deiring, was sunk in Kiel harbour to be raised and sunk again in its short life of less than a year. Lying here in a floating dry dock like a stranded whale, it could just as well have been one of the many boats which were scuttled towards the end of the war.

The North Sea coast was so shallow that considerable local knowledge was required to scuttle in the right places from where crews could reach dry land. Deep channels through these coastal waters are rare and in 1945 many of these still served as vital communications arteries for the small coastal communities. Therefore, blocking them with sunken ships could have presented more problems than it solved. What is more, tides force powerful currents along the coasts, which could easily wash small boats out to sea or allow waves to smash them on the shallows. In the end it was decided not to risk the lives of men in this way. Instead the few U-boats in Wilhelmshaven were scuttled inside one of the massive sea locks leading into the floating dock. Boats were driven in, scuttled and the locks filled to capacity with water before the control system was rendered inoperable.

Men living in Wilhelmshaven were told to take home everything they could use and everything else was thrown out of the windows of the base for locals to pick up. This resulted in the blue and white chequered naval bed linen becoming the basis of the first postwar fashions. Converted into women's clothing, the results became known as 'Dönitz dresses'. While this was going on, groups of trustworthy sailors were instructed to arm themselves and destroy all alcohol, including the stocks held in the bars in town. The reason was that the naval leadership feared a potential calamity being sparked off

Above: The beach at Habernis on the shores of Geltringer Bay where many U-boats and several ships were scuttled at the end of the war. A number of torpedo boats were required to bring valuable goods from U-boats ashore. This shows one which got stuck in the shallows and ended the war by being beached.

Above: No one in the small and isolated farms along the edge of Geltringer Bay knew that it had been chosen for scuttling U-boats and a number of curious children appeared on the beach when they spotted submarines and their supporting craft out at sea.

Above and overleaf: None of the Germans knew for how long they would be free from enemy interference and therefore the unloading and scuttling process had to be carried out at the double. What is more, there was hardly time to discuss the plans in detail. Improvisation, with everybody doing their best to help, was the order of the day. Once under way the process ran exceedingly well, with goods being moved away from the beach on carts borrowed from local farms.

by drunken Germans driving incoming troops into unnecessary retaliation. As things turned out, everything remained calm and it was just a case of locking the dockyard gates and waiting for the Allies to arrive.

In Kiel things were different. Not only was this base further away from the advancing armies but it also offered far more facilities for hiding U-boats away from the naval dockyard. Skeleton crews usually took them into sheltered deepwater bays where they lay submerged rather than being moored on the surface as targets for bombers. Exactly how the events of the last few days of war were organised has hardly been recorded, but the results were devastating and impressive. Virtually every floating ship was moved to be scuttled. Some boats were in such poor mechanical state or lacking the necessary fuel that they had to be sunk where they were, but a conglomeration of well over 50 assembled in Flensburger Förde, where most were scuttled in the shallow waters of Geltringer Bay. This was a good location because it was deep enough to hide the boats but well enough away from shipping routes not to hinder access to any port.

Although the operation ran relatively smoothly, *U1168* under Kptlt Hans Umlauf ran aground and had to be pulled free before reaching the destination, then the same boat struck once more on a shallow spot in the approaches to the bay. This time it was decided to blow it up where it was, leaving the hulk as a prominent memorial for some years to come. Others were even worse off. Kptlt Friedrich-Georg Herrle and Bootsmaat Schneider of *U393*, for example, were killed during an air attack just one day before the surrender came into effect and Obermaschinist Wilhelm Hegenbart of *U349* (ObltzS Wolfgang Dähne) chose to end his own life on board. His family and house had been destroyed during air raids, meaning that the U-boat had been his only home for the last months. Since there was no one left and nowhere to go, he wrapped himself in the battle ensign and detonated the scuttling charges.

Both *U1168* and *U393* were Type VIICs, which had been obsolete for some time, despite their later modifications, meaning there was no point in attempting to preserve them. Many of the other boats assembling in Geltringer Bay were the revolutionary Type XXI and XXIII electro-boats as well as some even more innovative craft. Sinking these was a little more complicated because it was thought that they might be required again in the not too distant future. There were rumours of co-operation with the Western Allies to drive the Russians out of Europe, but these pipe dreams never materialised. The care taken in scuttling some of these more modern craft can be illustrated by the fact that some of those boats were later raised to be made ready again in a very short period of time for the new Federal German Navy.

Above: There were hardly any landing stages and for most people it was a case of getting their feet wet. Some were lucky to get a lift over the last few metres. The stranded *U1168* can be made out in the distance above his head. The fact that he is wearing a white cap would suggest that he was a U-boat commander.

Kptlt Peter-Ottmar Grau was the Senior Officer for Submarines in Geltringer Bay. Fifteen months earlier he had commissioned *U872*, a long-range Type IXD2, and had prepared it for a voyage to the Far East when the last-minute finishing off work at Deschimag Works in Bremen was wrecked by an air raid. Luckily, only one man was killed when the boat went down by the side of the pier. Following this, Grau and the majority of his crew were given one of the first Type XXIs. Scuttling it less than five months after the commissioning was a solemn but rapid affair. Grau assembled his men and told them the reason for seeking refuge in the isolated North German bay. At the same time, he made it clear that in future they would have to be self-sufficient but, as long as stocks lasted, their stores should be used to alleviate the shortages on land. He pointed out that the small local population had grown quite dramatically by an influx of refugees from the eastern provinces, who had arrived after having lost virtually everything during their harrowing evacuation.

Hardly any of the men knew the spot where they were landing. Today, Geltringer Bay is a rather overcrowded holiday destination, but in those days of 1945 it could just as well have been at the end of the earth. The road to Flensburg, the nearest large town, was part cobblestones and part dirt track without signposts and the only fast communication with the rest of Germany was one single public telephone in a farmhouse. There was also an aircraft observation station with lookout tower, but this was so insignificant and isolated that the men could almost guarantee not being interrupted by the enemy while they unloaded their goods. Much of this was quite a straightforward process of filling inflatables, paddling them

ashore and dumping everything on the beach while others moved the goods by horse and cart to the nearby farms.

One major advantage of the isolation was that the people there had not been oppressed by the rules of war as much as town dwellers and usually listened to the Allied radio news as well as German stations. Consequently they could inform Grau of the advancing Allied army's position. This made it clear that it would be at least a day or two before they would have to worry about any interference from the land.

After unloading stores and scuttling boats, the next step was to collect weapons. The locals even surrendered their hunting guns. They had heard that entire farms had been burned down by the British because shotguns had been discovered inside them. Nobody wanted to give the troops an excuse to destroy their homes. In fact, although keen to disarm the German military, the occupying forces suggested that officers in Wilhelmshaven should carry guns again to prevent any trouble. However, no one fancied becoming the target for trigger-happy revolutionaries and the offer was declined with the suggestion that the Allies do their own shooting. Men wanted to go home and saw no reason to carry weapons any longer.

The surrender of the German forces in the north came into effect at 08.00hrs on 5 May. That first day of peace passed uneventfully, but the process of unloading the U-boats had been hard physical work and the men were pleased to seek out whatever accommodation the few farmhouses could offer. For the majority it was nothing more that snuggling up in a hay loft, but at least they knew that they had reached the bottom of the abyss and from then on everything had to get better. The anticipated influx of foreign soldiers did not materialise and the men along the shores of Geltringer Bay found that there was no interruption of their peaceful isolation. They knew that the British had reached the nearby towns, but nothing stirred out in the lonely farming communities. A good number of the men felt that they would stand a better chance of reaching home on their own, rather than remaining together as a large group. Consequently they said their farewells and, with tears in their eyes, departed to walk across the rolling fields of Schleswig-Holstein. A couple of weeks later a flotilla of torpedo boats arrived to take the rest of the men to Flensburg, from where they were herded into prison camps.

The waiting time was put to good use by seeing to the distribution of stores and making containers to carry personal luggage back home. Having been loaned an old but well-built sewing machine, the men set up a production line for the manufacture of haversacks. A war correspondent, Walter Schöppe, fell in love with one of the farmer's daughters and remained there to marry her and help run the farm.

The locals also made good use of the scuttled ships and submarines out in the bay. A number of them had gone down in such shallow water that parts remained above the waterline, offering welcome opportunities for salvaging everything which could be removed. The shortages of war and the excruciating hardships which were to follow made this a desirable addition to people's income, as well as providing a dangerous but fascinating playground for youngsters who could handle small boats.

Although many U-boats were scuttled along the Baltic shores, away from the main shipbuilding or naval centres, only two U-boats sought refuge in the dangerous shallows of the North Sea coast and both these were scuttled a considerable time after the end of the war. U287 (ObltzS Heinrich Meyer) left Norway a week before the end of the war for operations in the North Atlantic. The order to surrender by hoisting a black flag and then running on the surface into the nearest Allied port did not appeal. Instead the men chose to ignore the instructions and make their own way back home to Germany. Running into the Elbe estuary on 16 May, eleven days after the surrender had come into effect, they were unloaded in two locations along the northern shore while the commander, engineering officer and second watch officer drove on alone until they scuttled U287 on the southern shore, close to Altenbruch where the U-Boot-Archiv is now located. The reason for this elaborate procedure was to give everybody a better chance of getting home without a spell in prison camp first. It was hoped that the boat might not be discovered for some time but, if it was, then at least the majority of crew would be a good distance from the spot where the authorities were likely to start looking for them.

U979 (Kptlt Johannes Meermeier) was even further away, off Iceland, when the order to surrender came through. Again, no one on board fancied the idea of languishing in a prisoner of war camp and it was decided to outsmart the Allies by returning secretly to Germany. It was obvious to everybody that the naval bases and the major towns would be occupied and that they stood a better chance of staying free by making for isolated coastal communities from where they could disperse quietly and secretly back to their homes. Unfortunately, this plan was frustrated by turbulent currents. Running aground a good distance from land at low water with an ebbing tide meant there was no other choice than to paddle onto the sandbanks and then walk over the mud to the nearest habitation. There was still sufficient ammunition on board totally to destroy the boat on 24 May, almost three weeks after the end of the war, a defiant act against the surrender. The wreck, off Wittdünn on the island of Amrum, was still visible at extreme low tide during the mid-1990s.

Below: It could well be that this photograph was taken shortly before the torpedo boats took the U-boat men back to Flensburg, but the scene before the U-boats were scuttled would have looked fairly similar. Those wooden carts were still the mainstay for moving agricultural goods for many years after the war. Modern mechanisation did not make an impact until much later.

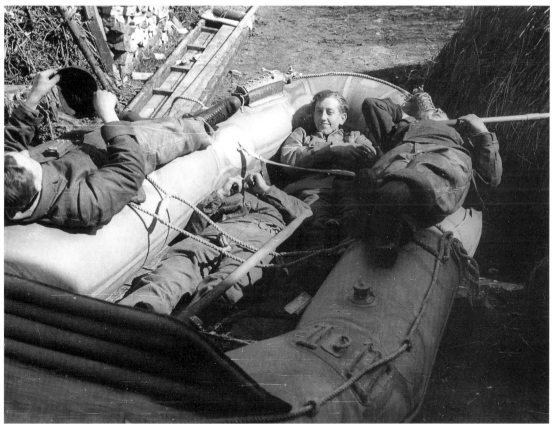

Above: Arms and ammunition were collected together for handing over to the Allied army of occupation whenever it arrived. This shows just a small corner of what became a considerable arsenal on the shores of Geltringer Bay. One wonders how much these items would fetch on the modern collectors' market.

Left: Emptying ships and U-boats, scuttling them and storing or distributing the goods was hard work. Having completed the tasks, men collapsed where they stood, to fill their bodies with new energy by sleeping.

Opposite & above: Having come to terms with the fact that the war was over, there was very little the men could do other than wait, but boredom was something U-boat men had got used to because much of their time was spent waiting for something to happen.

Right: Realising that the expected army of occupation was not going to rush in and herd everybody off to the horrors of prison camps, men started using the time for gainful activities. They borrowed an old but sturdy sewing machine to make haversacks to carry home the few personal possessions they had with them.

Right: Sitting and wearing the blue jumper is Kptlt Peter-Ottmar Grau. Having joined the navy in 1934, one year after Hitler had come to power, he was the senior officer along the shores of Geltringer Bay.

Above: Walter Schöppe, who took this sequence of photographs along the shores of Geltringer Bay, wrote the following inscription on the back of the picture: 'Then one day I came to say goodbye to the village. Kptlt Peter-Ottmar Grau, Kptlt Jürgen Klasing, Kptlt(Ing) Hilbig, Oberstabarzt Dr Klaus Täger, farmer Nicolaus Lassen, Mrs Jensen, Lenchen Lassen, Larga Lassen, Gerhard Enders, Friedrich Thormann, Mrs Thormann, Elizabeth Lassen, Günther Pleitz, Christel Thormann, Peter Jensen and Gabie Jensen have positioned themselves for a farewell photograph.'

Left: It was a case of getting dressed and ready to depart.

Above: The last parade by the farm at Habernis with Peter-Ottmar Grau addressing the men while everybody was being watched by a group of inquisitive children. The farmhouse in the background clearly shows that the muscle power for general maintenance had been missing for some time, with very little having been done to re-thatch the roof.

Above: With walking sticks in fashion, cherry blossom on the trees and accompanied by the younger members of the tiny farming community on the shores of the Geltringer Bay, U-boat men leave to become prisoners of war and then to contribute towards the building of a better and hopefully more peaceful Europe.

U-boats which Landed on or Approached Close to Foreign Shores

It is not claimed that this list is complete and some categories, such as boats which operated in shallow waters during the Norwegian campaign of spring 1940, boats which laid mines close to harbours, boats which landed in the Far East in Japanese-controlled ports and boats which surrendered in the United States after the end of the war, have been omitted.

Each boat number is followed by its type and the name of its commander.

U25 IA Viktor Schütze
The first U-boat of the war to refuel in Spain, from *Thalia* in Cadiz on 30 January 1940.

Above: Probably *U30*, showing the typical long and narrow bows of a Type VII. The large lumps in the jumping wire running up to the top of the conning tower are insulators to prevent the middle section, which also serves as radio aerial, from earthing with the boat. The head of the electric winch can be seen slightly towards the right. Poles could be inserted in the top to turn it manually if there was a power failure.

U29 VIIA Otto Schuhart
Refuelled in Vigo (Spain) from *Bessel* on 20 June 1940.

U30 VIIA Fritz-Julius Lemp
Landed wounded crewman in Reykjavik (Iceland) on 19 September 1939.
Refuelled in El Ferrol (Spain) from *Max Albrecht* on 4 June 1940. Was the first U-boat to be refuelled in a French Atlantic port when it put in to Lorient on 7 July 1940.

U35 VIIA Werner Lott
Landed 28 merchant seamen from SS *Diamantis* in Ventry Bay (Ireland) on 3 or 4 October 1939. The departure of the boat was watched by a large number of locals, waving from the shore. The 4,990grt *Diamantis* was sunk by *U35* at 13.50hrs on 3 October 1939 some 75km west of the Skelligs.

U37 IXA Werner Hartmann
Landed an agent in Donegal Bay (Ireland) on 8 February 1940.
Possibly undertook a special mission to French West Africa during December 1940.

U38 IXA Heinrich Liebe
Landed two agents in Ireland on 12 June 1940.
Carried out a reconnaissance of Norwegian and Soviet coasts in November and December 1939.

U43 IXA Wilhelm Ambrosius
Refuelled in Vigo from *Bessel* on 18 June 1940.
Was supposed to have landed an agent but reliable records verifying that this was carried out have not been found.

U52 VIIB Otto Salmann
Refuelled in Vigo from *Bessel* on 1 July 1940.

U65 IXB Hans-Gerrit von Stockhausen
Left for a mission to land two agents in Ireland. One agent died en route and the boat returned. Von Stockhausen was killed a short while later in a road accident in Berlin.

U66 IXC Friedrich Markworth
Refuelled in El Ferrol from *Max Albrecht* on 17 May 1942.
Landed an agent near Cape Blanc in Mauritania, close to the border with Spanish Sahara, on 20/21 January 1943. Agent and two of the crew were captured.

U67 IXC Günter Müller-Stöckheim
28 October 1941, met *U111* in Tarafel Bay (Cape Verde Islands) to refuel from *U68*. The three boats were surprised by HM Submarine *Clyde*.
16 February 1942, attacked ships lying at anchor off Curaçao (Caribbean) and later joined forces with *U502* to shell oil installations on Aruba.

U68 IXC Karl-Friedrich Merten
Refuelled in El Ferrol from *Max Albrecht* on 17 May 1942. Also see *U67*.

U69 VIIC Jost Metzler
Refuelled in Las Palmas (Canary Islands) from *Charlotte Schliemann* on 30 June 1941.
Attacked shipping at anchor in several African harbours.

U73 VIIB Horst Deckert
Landed an agent in Algeria during the night of 9/10 October 1943.

U77 VIIC Heinrich Schonder
Refuelled in Vigo from *Bessel* on 7 November 1941.

U81 VIIC Friedrich Guggenberger
Bombarded a power station in Palestine on 17 April 1942 and it is likely that the boat also shelled oil tanks near Haifa afterwards.

U83 VIIB Hans-Werner Kraus
Left for a special commando operation in the Gulf of Bomba (Cyrenaica) on 28 May 1942, but the attack was aborted due to technical problems.

U96 VIIC Heinrich Lehmann-Willenbrock
Refuelled in Vigo from *Bessel* on 27 November 1941 with the war correspondent Lothar-Günther Buchheim on board, who later wrote the novel *Das Boot*, which was made into the highly successful film of the same title.

U103 IXB Viktor Schütze
Refuelled in Las Palmas from *Charlotte Schliemann* on 5 July 1941.

U105 IXB Georg Schewe/Heinrich Schuch
Refuelled in Las Palmas from *Charlotte Schliemann* on 4 March 1941.
Was repaired in El Ferrol 12–28 June 1942.

U106 IXB Jürgen Oesten
Refuelled in Las Palmas from *Charlotte Schliemann* on 5 March 1941.

U109 IXB Heinrich Bleichrodt
Refuelled in Cadiz from *Thalia* on 21 July 1941.

U111 IXB Wilhelm Kleinschmidt
See *U67*.

U123 IXB Reinhard Hardegen
Refuelled in Las Palmas from *Charlotte Schliemann* on 25 June 1941.

U124 IXB Georg-Wilhelm Schultz
Refuelled in Las Palmas from *Charlotte Schliemann* on 3 March 1941.

U130 IXC Ernst Kals
Fired 12 shells at oil installations near Curaçao on 19 April 1942 before being driven off by gunfire from the land.

U155 IXC Ludwig von Friedeburg
9 September 1944, was the last boat to be evacuated from Lorient in France under LtzS Friedeburg who was the youngest person to command a U-boat.

U156 IXC Werner Hartenstein
Tried to bombard oil installations on Aruba on 16 February 1942 without first removing the watertight tampion from the end of the gun barrel. This resulted in one death and the gunnery officer being seriously injured. He was put ashore at Fort de France on Martinique on 18 February.

U161 IXC Albrecht Achilles
Attacked ships made fast to a pier at Puerto Limón (Costa Rica) during the night of 2-3 July 1942.

U167 IXC Kurt Sturm
Scuttled near Gran Canaria on 6 April 1943.

U186 IXC Siegfried Hesemann
Carried out a brief reconnaissance of fjords in Greenland during January 1942.

U193 IXC Hans Pauckstadt
Damaged in Bay of Biscay by aircraft on 9 February 1944. Put in to El Ferrol during the following day to repair the damage. Left again on 20 February to arrive in Lorient on the 24th.

U200 IXD2 Heinrich Schonder
Lost to air attack on 24 June 1943 near Reykjavik (Iceland) with seven men of a special assault group from the Brandenburg Division on board.

U202 VIIC Hans-Heinz Linder
Landed agents on Long Island (USA) on 13 June 1942.

U204 VIIC Walter Kell
Refuelled in Cadiz from *Thalia* on 15 October 1941.

U205 VIIC Friedrich Bürgel
Was damaged in the eastern Mediterranean, abandoned and then towed to North Africa by HMS *Gloxinia*, but sank in deep water within sight of land.

U209 VIIC Heinrich Brodda
Shelled a radio station with *U255* at Cape Zhelania on 25 August 1942 and another radio station at Khodovarikha on 28 August, both on Novaya Zemlya.

U212 VIIC Helmut Vogler
Landed reconnaissance troops on Bear Island to destroy the remains of an Allied weather station in June 1943.

U213 VIID Amelung von Varendorff
Landed an agent near Saint John (New Brunswick, Canada) on 14 May 1942.

U217 VIID Kurt Reichenbach-Klinke
Attacked a ship lying at anchor off Willemstadt (Curaçao) on 19 August 1942.

U242 VIIC Heinrich Riedel
Landed an agent in Finland on 23 January 1945 and then carried out a reconnaissance of the Gulf of Bothnia.

Above: U223, a typical Type VIIC, showing what the boat looked like from a dinghy.

Above: U255 under Kptlt Reinhard Reche during the autumn of 1943, refuelling a Blohm und Voss reconnaissance plane in the Kara Sea. The land in the background is reputed to be part of Novaya Zemlya.

U252 VIIC Kai Lerchen
Landed an agent in Iceland on 6 April 1942.

U255 VIIC Reinhard Reche/Erich Harms
Special mission to refuel a Blohm und Voss 138 flying boat while on general reconnaissance in the Arctic during August 1942.
25 August 1942, shelled two radio stations with *U209*. See *U209*.
1 August 1943, established a radio station near Spoyj Navolok on Novaya Zemlya and refuelled a Blohm und Voss 138 flying boat to carry out a reconnaissance of Wilkitski Strait.

U255 was lying in St Nazaire (France) after the town was surrounded by Allied armies. There it was supplied with fuel from *U878* and eventually made its way to La Pallice and back again to St Nazaire. These precarious voyages took place in shallow waters towards the last days of the war.

U260 VIIC Klaus Becker
Was mined off Ireland on 12 March 1945. Forty-eight men made their own way ashore to be interned.

U262 VIIC Heinz Franke
Reached North Point on Prince Edward Island on 2 May 1943 to pick up escapees from a prisoner of war camp near Fredericton, but the escape did not take place and *U262* returned empty-handed. This voyage was mentioned in my book *U-boat Commanders and Crews 1939-45*, although I wrongly identified the boat there as *U292*.

U279 VIIC Otto Finke
Landed an agent in Iceland in September 1943 and was sunk shortly afterwards. There were no survivors.

U287 VIIC Heinrich Meyer
Scuttled in the Elbe estuary near Cuxhaven-Altenbruch, where the U-Boot-Archiv is now located.

U289 VIIC Alexander Hellwig
Special operation 24–26 April 1944 near Heradsfloi (Iceland).

U302 VIIC Herbert Sickel
Rescued the weather team *Nussbaum* from Spitzbergen 20–24 June 1943. This involved a clash with a Norwegian gunboat.

U307 VIIC Friedrich-Georg Herrle
Landed on Spitzbergen on 15 September 1944 to help set up a manned weather station and to carry out a general reconnaissance.

U331 VIIC Freiherr Hans-Diedrich von Tiesenhausen
Refuelled in Cadiz from *Thalia* 1 August 1941.
Landed commando troops in North Africa between Tobruk and El Alamein during the night of 17/18 November 1941, shortly before sinking the British battleship HMS *Barham*.

Below: U302 which rescued members of the *Nussbaum* weather team from Spitzbergen.

Above: U302 close to Narvik in northern Norway, one of the main bases for boats operating in the Arctic.

Above: U302 with the early type of conning tower which accommodated a single 20mm anti-aircraft gun.

Above: A temporary camp set up on Spitzbergen by *U307* under Friedrich-Georg Herrle.

Right: ObltzS Herrle on the conning tower of *U307*. There is a twin 20mm anti-aircraft gun towards the right.

Above: U307 with ObltzS Herrle talking to the Norwegian radio operator Börgesen prior to helping him establish a secret base on Spitzbergen.

Above: U307 with men having shot reindeer for fresh meat to supplement their diet.

Above: U307 with the later type of conning tower holding the strengthened anti-aircraft armament.

Above: *U307* in Eisfjord on Spitzbergen. The circular aerial of a radar detector can be seen towards the right-hand edge of the conning tower.

Right: *U351*, a typical Type VIIC, showing how low the bows cut through the water.

U371 under Hans-Joachim Neumann obviously in safe waters where a large number of men could be allowed out on deck.

Left: U377 under Kptlt Otto Köhler helping to establish a manned weather station on Cape Mitra on Spitzbergen.

Right: U377 at Cape Mitra (Spitzbergen). The men were fortunate that the fjord froze over, allowing them to unload the heavy gear by carrying it over the ice rather than paddling it ashore in inflatable dinghies.

Left: Unloading stores onto sledges from *U377* and dragging them over the ice. The T-shaped object on the bows is the head of early underwater sound detection gear.

Above: Men from *U377* carrying goods for the weather base at Cape Mitra across the ice.

Above: Men from *U377* carrying goods for the weather base at Cape Mitra across the ice.

U354 VIIC Karl-Heinz Herbschleb
Established a manned weather station on Hopen Island in October 1943.
Recovered the weather team from Hopen Island in July 1944. Established a manned weather station *Svartisen* on Hopen Island in October 1944, shortly after *U703* had evacuated shipwrecked Russians from the island. This team was evacuated again by *U354* on 22 July 1944.

U355 VIIC Günter La Baume
Destroyed an abandoned Allied weather station on Spitzbergen in July 1943.
6 October 1943, approached Spitzbergen to help set up a manned weather station and to carry out a general reconnaissance.

U365 VIIC Heimar Wedemeyer
Landed weather team on Spitzbergen in October 1944.

U370 VIIC Karl Nielsen
Helped to evacuate a German radio station from Finland on 3 September 1944.

U372 VIIC Hans-Joachim Neumann
Left for a mission to land an agent in Beirut (Lebanon) but was sunk on 27 July 1942 before this mission could be carried out. The crew and the agent survived.

U377 VIIC Otto Köhler
Landed several times on Spitzbergen to set up an automatic weather station, to help establish a manned weather station and to carry out a general reconnaissance of the Cape Mitra area to the northwest. This took place during the summer and autumn of 1942.
January 1943, made an unsuccessful attempt to penetrate into the Royal Navy's anchorage at Scapa Flow (Orkney Islands).

U38 VIIC Josef Röther
Set out to supply the Afrika Korps with ammunition and rescued four German soldiers from Tunisia on 10 May 1943.

U387 VIIC Rudolf Büchler
Sailed into the polar seas with the weather ship *Kehdingen* to establish a manned weather base on Franz Josef Land towards the end of September 1943.
Landed Prince George's Island, Novaya Zemlya to the north of Russia, to set up an automatic land-based weather station in October 1944. (Prince George's Island has often been confused with a location in Canada.)

U434 VIIC Wolfgang Heyda
Refuelled in Vigo from *Bessel* on 14 December 1941.

U435 VIIC Siegfried Strelow
Carried out a reconnaissance of Spitzbergen and landed the weather team *Knospe* in August 1942. Probably also evacuated men from Cape Mitra on Spitzbergen later in the month.

U502 IXC Jürgen von Rosenstiel
See *U67*.

U513 IXC Rolf Rüggeberg
Attacked shipping anchored in Conception Bay (Canada) and sunk the ore carriers *Lord Strathcona* and *Saranga* in daylight on 5 September 1942.

U515 IXC Werner Henke
Was repaired off the Canary Islands 21–25 November 1940, but the men probably did not go ashore.

U517 IXC Paul Ludwig
11–15 September 1942, entered the estuary of the St Lawrence River (Canada) to attack shipping.

U518 IXC Friedrich-Wilhelm Wissmann
Landed agent near New Brunswick to make his way to Quebec (Canada) on 9 November 1942.

U530 IXC Otto Wermuth
Met Japanese submarine *I.52* to transfer technicians and radar equipment plus an interpreter-cum-pilot for taking the boat into Lorient in June 1944. Wermuth refused to surrender at the end of the war and took his boat to Argentina, where it arrived on 10 July 1945. The boat was subsequently handed over to the United States, while the men were interned.

Above: U405 under Kptlt Rolf-Heinrich Hopman exploring one of the wrecks from the bitter fighting around Narvik in Norway.

Below: A long-range U-boat at sea.

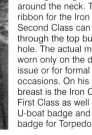

Above: Siegfried Stehlow of *U435*, who carried out a reconnaissance of Spitzbergen and landed a weather team there. He is wearing a Knight's Cross around the neck. The ribbon for the Iron Cross Second Class can be seen through the top button hole. The actual medal was worn only on the day of issue or for formal occasions. On his left breast is the Iron Cross First Class as well as a U-boat badge and the badge for Torpedo Boats.

U536 IXC Rolf Schauenburg
Attempted to pick up escaped prisoners of war from
Maisonette Point, Chaleur Bay (Canada) 3–5 October 1943.

U537 IXC Peter Schrewe
Established an automatic unmanned weather station at Martin
Bay, Labrador (Canada) 22–23 October 1943.

U541 IXC Kurt Petersen
13 September 1944, entered the estuary of the St Lawrence to
attack shipping. Dived under ice and later surfaced to recharge
batteries by breaking through a thin patch in a large sheet
of ice.

U553 VIIC Karl Thurmann
The first U-boat to penetrate into the estuary of the
St Lawrence during May 1942.

U564 VIIC Reinhard Suhren
Refuelled in Cadiz from *Thalia* 14 October 1941.

U566 VIIC Hans Hornkohl
Damaged by aircraft on 24 October 1943 and scuttled off
Spain. The crew were rescued by Spanish fishermen and taken
to Vigo. From there they travelled by train to Brest, had some
home leave and then commissioned *U1007*.

U573 VIIC Heinrich Heinsohn
Damaged by aircraft on 1 May 1942 and then reached
Cartagena (Spain) under its own power. The boat was later
sold to Spain and saw service as *G7* until 1970.

U574 VIIC Dietrich Gengelbach
Refuelled in Vigo from *Bessel* on 11 December 1941.

U575 VIIC Günther Heydemann
Refuelled in Vigo from *Bessel* on 12 December 1941.

U581 VIIC Werner Pfeiffer
Was depth charged and sunk very close to the Azores by HMS
Westcott (Cdr I. H. Bockett-Pugh). Four men died, one man
escaped by swimming ashore and the rest were captured to
become prisoners of war.

U584 VIIC Joachim Deecke
Landed agents in Florida (USA) on 17 June 1942.

U586 VIIC Dietrich von der Esch
Carried out a reconnaissance of Jan Mayen in October 1942.

U587 VIIC Ulrich Borcherdt
Fired torpedoes into the harbour at St John's (Newfoundland)
on 3 March 1942 but did not sink anything.

U593 VIIC Gerd Kelbling
Undertook a special mission to Sicily during July–August
1943.

U595 VIIC Jürgen Quaet-Faslem
Beached near Ténès (Algeria) on 14 November 1943 after
secrets had been destroyed.

U601 VIIC Peter-Ottmar Grau
Set up a weather station on Novaya Zemlya during August 1943.

Above: Probably *U617* under Albrecht Brandi with Mediterranean type of
camouflage. This was a standard Type VIIC from Blohm und Voss in
Hamburg. The attack periscope has been raised to act as flagpole. The
snorting bull of Scapa Flow painted on the conning tower was originally the
emblem of *U47*. Before sailing into the Mediterranean, *U617* belonged to the
7th U-Flotilla, which had adopted that emblem when *U47* was lost.

U617 VIIC Albrecht Brandi
Damaged by aircraft and beached on the coast of Spanish
Morocco on 12 September 1943. The boat was bombarded by
the Royal Navy to prevent it leaving again. Some men escaped
to make their way back to Germany, but the majority were
interned in Spain. Mentioned briefly in my book *Enigma
U-boats* (Ian Allan Publishing, 2000).

U629 VIIC Hans-Helmuth Bugs
Set up an automatic weather station on Bear Island on 6 July
1943.

U636 VIIC Eberhard Schendel
Established a manned weather station on Hopen Island
9–14 October 1944. It is likely that the boat evacuated other
weathermen from Hopen Island at the same time.
Supplied a weather team on Spitzbergen with provisions on
10 December 1944.

U652 VIIC Georg-Werner Fraatz
Was refuelled in Cadiz from *Thalia* on 27 November 1941.

U657 VIIC Heinrich Göllnitz
Set up an automatic weather station on Bear Island
30 November–2 December 1942.

U668 VIIC Wolfgang von Eickstedt
Evacuated one man from a weather detachment on Bear Island
on 10 April 1945. The other member of this two-man team
failed to return from a hunting trip on the island and was
presumed to have died.

U703 VIIC Joachim Brünner
Undertook a reconnaissance of Hopen Island in July 1943 and
found four Russian survivors from a ship sunk nine months
earlier.
Set up an automatic weather station on Novaya Zemlya in
August 1943.

U711 VIIC Hans-Günther Lange
Shelled radio station on Nansen Island and at Blagopoluchia
on Novaya Zemlya in September 1943 together with *U739*
and *U957*.

U713 VIIC Henri Gosejacob
Set up a weather station on Bear Island on 29 November
1943.

Below: U617 after having been stranded in North Africa as a result of severe
damage caused by attacks from two Wellington bombers, piloted by
D. Hodgkinson and W. Brunini.

U722 VIIC Hans-Heinrich Reimers
Undertook a cargo-carrying mission to supply St Nazaire from
Norway during October 1944.

U737 VIIC Paul Brasack
Set up a weather station on Bear Island during August 1943.
Carried out a general reconnaissance of Spitzbergen in
October 1943.
Set up an automatic weather station on Bear Island on 17 June
1944.
Evacuated a weather team from Spitzbergen on 30 June 1944
and set up an automatic weather station at around the same
time. The leader of the team, which had over-wintered,
H. R. Knoespel, was killed by a mine explosion shortly before
the pick-up.
Landed on Bear Island on 6 July 1944 to check an automatic
weather station already installed there.

U739 VIIC Ernst Mangold
Shelled a Russian radio station on Novaya Zemlya
24–26 September 1944 with *U711* and *U957*.

U741 VIIC Gerhard Palmgren
Attempted to re-supply Cherbourg during June 1944, but the
city fell while under way and the mission was aborted.

U760 VIIC Otto-Ulrich Blum
Damaged by aircraft on 6–7 August 1943 and towed into
Vigo where the crew was interned.

This page and opposite top: The narrows between HMS *Dolphin*, the Royal Navy's submarine school on the right and Portsmouth on the left, looking out towards the waters of Spithead where *U763* (Ernst Cordes) ended up accidentally as a result of an intensive depth charge attack. Luckily for the Germans, they succeeded in extracting themselves without drawing attention to their plight.

Above: Landing on foreign shores was not the sole prerogative of U-boat men. Auxiliary cruisers also called on numerous isolated islands. This shows men from the ghost cruiser *Pinguin* (KptzS Ernst-Felix Krüder) on Kerguelen in the deep southern reaches of the Indian Ocean.

U763 VIIC Ernst Cordes
An attack of over 350 depth charges during the night of 8/9 July 1944 forced *U763* accidentally into Spithead, between Portsmouth and the Isle of Wight (England). The crew managed to extract themselves without drawing attention to their plight.

U852 IXD2 Heinz-Wilhelm Eck
Beached on the Somalian coast of East Africa on 3 May 1944, after damage by aircraft. This is mentioned in my book *Enigma U-boats*.

U862 IXD2 Heinrich Timm
Sailed within sight of New Zealand in January 1945. Although there are tales of men having gone ashore, none of them actually landed.

U867 IXC Arved von Mühlendahl
Was sunk on 18 September 1944 while transporting an automatic weather station for installation in Labrador.

U868 IXC Eduart Türre
Undertook a cargo-carrying supply mission to St Nazaire 21 January — 9 April 1945, returning to Norway just a few weeks before the end of the war.

U878 IXC Johannes Rodig
Undertook a cargo-carrying supply mission from Norway to St Nazaire, but was sunk on 10 April 1945 during the return journey. Refuelled *U255* in St Nazaire.

U956 VIIC Hans-Dieter Mohs
Mined Novaya Zemlya and escorted the weather observation ship *Hessen*. Might have landed in the Arctic.

U957 VIIC Gerd Schaar
Destroyed Russian radio station on Novaya Zemlya 24–26 September 1944 together with *U711* and *U739*.

U955 VIIC Hans-Heinrich Baden
Landed agents in Iceland on 30 April 1944.

U960 VIIC Günter Heinrich
Might have landed on Novaya Zemlya.

U965 VIIC Günter Unverzagt
Escorted the Weather Observation Ship *Externsteine* to Alexandra Land (northern Russia) for setting up a weather station in October 1944.

U966 VIIC Eckehard Wolf
Damaged by aircraft off Spain and later scuttled. Some of the crew were rescued by Spanish fishermen, while others made their own way ashore.

U977 VIIC Heinz Schäfer
Landed 16 men near Bergen shortly after the end of the war and then sailed to Argentina where the remaining men surrendered on 17 August 1945.

U979 VIIC Johannes Meermeier
Scuttled near the North Friesian island of Amrum shortly after the end of the war.

U992 VIIC Hans Falke
Set up an automatic weather station on Jan Mayen and later supplied a weather station on Bear Island. It is possible that the boat called twice at Jan Mayen, on 17 July 1944 and on 25 September 1944.

U994 VIIC Volker Melzer
Was due to have established an automatic weather station on Bear Island in April 1945, but the war ended before these plans could be put into operation.

U995 VIIC Hans-Georg Hess
Landed a reconnaissance party on Litzki Island on 23 December 1944.

U1163 VIIC Ernst-Ludwig Balduhn
Set up a weather station in northern Norway on 11 November 1944 and another on Bear Island 16–20 November 1944.

U1209 VIIC Ewald Hülsenbeck
Ran aground near the Wolf Rock Lighthouse (near Land's End, England) and sank on 26 November 1944.

U1229 IXC Armin Zinke
Was on the way to land the agent Oskar Mantel in the United States, but was sunk on 20 August 1944 before the mission could be carried out.

U1230 IXC Hans Hilbig
Landed two agents in the Gulf of Maine 29-30 November 1944.

Further Reading

Busch, Rainer and Röll, Hans-Joachim, *Der U-Boot-Krieg 1939 bis 1945*. Vol 1, *Die deutschen U-Boot-Kommandanten*, Koehler/Mittler, Hamburg, Berlin, Bonn, 1996. Published in English by Greenhill as *U-boat Commanders*. (Brief biographies produced from the records of the German U-Boot-Archiv. Sadly, the English edition has been published without the numerous corrections recorded by the Archive.)

Busch, Rainer and Röll, Hans-Joachim, *Der U-Boot-Krieg 1939-1945*, E. S. Mittler & Sohn, Hamburg, Berlin and Bonn, 1999. German U-boat losses from September 1939 to May 1945 from the records of the U-Boot-Archiv.

Compton-Hall, Richard, *The Underwater War 1939–45*, Blanford, Poole, 1982. The author was formerly director of the Royal Navy's Submarine Museum and this is by far the best book for describing life in submarines.

Garlinski, Josef, *Intercept, The Enigma War*, J. M. Dent, London, 1979. Includes details of a number of U-boats which operated in British coastal waters, but this information does not correlate with U-boat Command records.

Gellermann, Günther W., *Der andere Auftrag*, Bernard & Graefe, Bonn, 1997. Interesting and detailed accounts about agents who were landed on foreign shores.

Gröner, Erich, *Die deutschen Kriegsschiffe 1815–1945*, J. F. Lehmanns, Munich, 1968. This is the standard book on the technical data of German warships. Much of the information is tabulated, making it relatively easy for non-German readers. However, the section dealing with U-boat losses contains a good proportion of questionable information.

Gröner, Erich, *Die Handelsflotten der Welt*, 1942, J. F. Lehmanns, Munich, reprinted 1976. Includes details of ships sunk up to 1942. This valuable publication was originally a confidential document and contains a complete list of ships, in similar style to Lloyd's *Register*. There is also a lengthy section with good line drawings.

Hadley, Michael L., *U-boats against Canada*, McGill-Queen's University Press, Kingston and Montreal, 1985. An excellent book which includes detailed information about U-boats which approached the Canadian coast.

Harbon, John D., *The Longest Battle: The RCN in the Atlantic 1939-1945* Vanwell, Ontario, 1993.

Herzog, Bodo, *60 Jahre deutsche Uboote 1906-1966*, J. F. Lehmanns, Munich, 1968. A useful book with much tabulated information.

Herzog, Bodo, *U-boats in Action*, Ian Allan, Shepperton and Podzun, Dorheim. A pictorial book with captions in English.

Hessler, Günter, Hoschatt, Alfred, and others, *The U-boat War in the Atlantic*, HMSO, 1989.

Hirschfeld, Wolfgang, *Feindfahrten*, Neff, Vienna, 1982. The secret diary of a U-boat radio operator compiled in the radio rooms of operational submarines. A most invaluable insight into the war and probably one of the most significant accounts of the war at sea.

Hirschfeld, Wolfgang, *Das Letzte Boot — Atlantik Farewell*, Universitas, Munich, 1989. The last journey of *U234*, surrender in the United States and life as a prisoner of war.

Hirschfeld, Wolfgang, and Brooks, Geoffrey, *Hirschfeld — The Story of a U-boat NCO 1940–46*, Leo Cooper, London, 1996. A fascinating English language edition of Hirschfeld's life in U-boats.

Högel, Georg, *Embleme Wappen Malings deutscher Uboote 1939-1945*, Koehlers, Hamburg, Berlin, Bonn, 1997. Published in English as *U-boat Emblems of World War II 1939-1945*, Schiffer Military History, Atglen, 1999. An excellent work dealing with U-boat emblems, especially those which were painted on conning towers. Very well illustrated with drawings by the author, who served in *U30* and *U110*.

Jung, D., Maass, M. and Wenzel, B., *Tanker und Versorger der deutschen Flotte 1900–1980*, Motorbuch, Stuttgart, 1981. This excellent book is the standard reference work on the German naval supply system.

Kemp, Paul, *U-boats Destroyed*, Arms and Armour, London, 1997.

Lohmann, W. and Hildebrand, H. H., *Die deutsche Kriegsmarine 1939–1945*, Podzun, Dorheim, 1956–64. This multi-volume work is the standard reference document on the German navy, giving details of ships, organisation and personnel.

Meister, Jürg, *Der Seekrieg in den osteuropäischen Gewässern 1941-1945*, J. F. Lehmanns, Munich, 1958.

Milner, Marc, *North Atlantic Run*, Naval Institute Press, Annapolis, 1985.

Möller, Eberhard, *Kurs Atlantik*, Motorbuch Verlag, Stuttgart, 1995.

Moore, Captain Arthur R., *A careless word . . . a needless sinking*, American Merchant Marine Museum, Maine, 1983. A detailed and well-illustrated account of ships lost during the war.

Mulligan, Timothy P., *Neither Sharks Nor Wolves*, United States Naval Institute Press, Annapolis, 1999 and Chatham Publishing, London, 1999. An excellent book about the men who manned the U-boats.

Niestle, Axel, *German U-boat Losses during World War II*, Greenhill, London, 1998.

Nusser, Franz, *Die Arktisunternehmen des deutschen Marinewetterdienstes in den Jahren 1940-45*, Deutscher Wetterdienst, Hamburg, 1979.

OKM (Supreme Naval Command), *Bekleidungs und Anzugsbestimmungen für die Kriegsmarine*, Berlin, 1935; reprinted Jak P. Mallmann Showell, 1979. The official dress regulations of the German navy.

OKM (Supreme Naval Command), *Rangliste der deutschen Kriegsmarine*, Mittler & Sohn, published annually, Berlin.

OKM (Supreme Naval Command), *Handbuch für U-boot-Kommandanten*, Berlin, 1942. Translated during the war and published by Thomas Publications, Gettysburg, 1989 as *The U-boat Commander's Handbook*.

Ritter, Christiane, *Eine Frau erlebt die Polarnacht*, Ullstein Verlag, Frankfurt, 1978. Translated into English as *A Woman in the Polar Night*.

Rohwer, J., *Axis Submarine Successes of World War II 1939-45*, Greenhill, London, 1998.

Rohwer, J., and Hümmelchen, G., *Chronology of the War at Sea 1939–1945*, Greenhill, London, 1992. A good, solid and informative work. Well-indexed and most useful for anyone studying the war at sea.

Roskill, Captain S. W., *The War at Sea*, HMSO, London, 1954, reprinted 1976. Four volumes. The British official history.

Rössler, Eberhard, *Die deutschen Uboote und ihre Werften*, Bernard & Graefe, Koblenz, 1979.

Rössler, Eberhard, *Geschichte des deutschen Ubootbaus*, Bernard & Graefe, Koblenz, 1986.

Rössler, Eberhard, *The U-boat*, Arms and Armour Press, London, 1981.

Selinger, Franz, *Abriss der Unternehmungen des Marinewetterdienstes in der Arktis 1940-45 nach dem Erkenntnisstand von 1990*, Deutscher Wetterdienst, Hamburg, 1991.

Sharpe, Peter, *U-boat Fact File*, Midland Publishing, Leicester, 1998.

Showell, Jak P. Mallmann, *The German Navy in World War Two*, Arms and Armour Press, London, 1979; Naval Institute Press, Annapolis, 1979 and translated as *Das Buch der deutschen Kriegsmarine*, Motorbuch Verlag, Stuttgart, 1982. Covers history, organisation, the ships, code writers, naval charts and a section on ranks, uniforms, awards and insignias by Gordon Williamson. Named by the United States Naval Institute as 'One of the Outstanding Naval Books of the Year'.

Showell, Jak P. Mallmann, *U-boats under the Swastika*, Ian Allan, Shepperton, 1973; Arco, New York, 1973 and translated as *Uboote gegen England*, Motorbuch, Stuttgart, 1974. A well-illustrated introduction to the German U-boat Arm, which is now one of the longest selling naval books in Germany.

Showell, Jak P. Mallmann, *U-boats under the Swastika*, Ian Allan, London, 1987. A second edition of the above title with different photos and new text.

Showell, Jak P. Mallmann, *U-boat Command and the Battle of the Atlantic*, Conway Maritime Press, London, 1989; Vanwell, New York, 1989. A detailed history based on the U-boat Command's war diary.

Showell, Jak P. Mallmann, *Germania International*, Journal of the German Navy Study Group. Now out of print.

Showell, Jak P. Mallmann, *U-boat Commanders and Crews*, The Crowood Press, Marlborough, 1998.

Showell, Jak P. Mallmann, *German Navy Handbook 1939–1945*, Sutton Publishing, Stroud, 1999.

Showell, Jak P. Mallmann, *U-boats in Camera 1939–1945*, Sutton Publishing, Stroud, 1999.

Showell, Jak P. Mallmann, *Enigma U-boats*, Ian Allan, London, 2000.

U-Boot-Archiv *Das Archiv*, (German) *The U-boat Archive* (English language). A journal published twice a year for members of FTU, U-Boot-Archiv, Bahnhofstrasse 57, D-27478 Cuxhaven-Altenbruch. Please enclose at least two International Postal Reply Coupons if asking for details.

Verband Deutscher Ubootsfahrer *Schaltung Küste*. Journal of the German Submariners' Association.

Wagner, Gerhard (editor), *Lagevorträge des Oberbefehlshabers der Kriegsmarine vor Hitler*, J.F. Lehmanns, Munich, 1972. Translated as *Fuehrer Conferences on Naval Affairs*, Greenhill, London, reprinted with new introduction 1990. The first English language edition was published before the German version.

Williamson, Gordon, and Pavlovik, Darko, *U-boat Crews 1914-45*, Osprey, London, 1995. A most interesting book with excellent colour drawings and black and white photographs.

Witthöft, Hans Jürgen, *Lexikon zur deutschen Marinegeschichte*, Koehler, Herford, 1977. An excellent two-volume encyclopaedia.

Wynn, Kenneth, *U-boat Operations of World War 2*, Chatham, London, 1997.

Index

Boats listed in the Appendix in numerical order have not been included in this index. References which occur more often in a chapter have only been indexed once.